Praise

"An insightful look into [...] [...] [...]ve're meant to do, and how to [...] [...] [...]until now, a lot of us have just [...] [...]"
—Bob Goff, *New York Times* bestselling author of *Love Does*

"Given the long struggle we have had in the U.S., to live to see justice return to the evangelical church, to have young pastors such as Palmer Chinchen calling for justice, is good news for the church in our day. I encourage you to read *Justice Calling*."
—John M. Perkins, cofounder of the Christian Community Development Association (CCDA), founder of the John M. Perkins and Vera Mae Foundation, and coauthor of *Making Neighborhoods Whole: A Handbook for Christian Community Development*

"Palmer Chinchen carries us far more than halfway toward the heart of God, in the pursuit of a world that loves mercy, does justice, and walks humbly."
—Erwin Raphael McManus, bestselling author and cultural architect

"*Justice Calling* is a challenge to leaders, the church, and our generation. To both 'be' and 'do' in a day when it's more important than ever that our actions, as followers of Jesus, line up with our thoughts and words. This book is a practical and helpful resource for understanding the importance of Justice."
—Brad Lomenick, founder of BLINC, author of *H3 Leadership* and *The Catalyst Leader*

"*Justice Calling* is a fresh reminder that we are called as followers of Jesus to make earth look more a little more like heaven. The words 'social justice' might sound intimidating to some, but that is truly what we get when we commit to serve others, and allow Jesus to shine through us."
—Jon Steingard, musician and frontman of Hawk Nelson

"Not only am I proud to call Palmer my friend, but his book *Justice Calling* is also a must-read for anyone who cares about social justice and growing their faith."

—Larry Fitzgerald, NFL wide receiver for the Arizona Cardinals, nine-time Pro Bowler

"*Justice Calling* is full of incredible stories of what God can do through us if we are willing to trust Him and go! We are called to take care of the widows and orphans, and those who cannot take care of themselves. I found this book not only encouraging but a challenge to authentically and passionately live out my faith through service."

—Adam Agee, musician and frontman of Audio Adrenaline

"This is a fearless book, and Palmer Chinchen is an authentic and courageous voice calling Christians not just to the journey inward but to the journey outward as well."

—Dr. Todd Pickett, Dean of Spiritual Development at Biola University

"Palmer Chinchen is a dear friend in Christ. I had the honor to be a part of *Barefoot Tribe*, and truly feel Palmer has knocked it out of the park with *Justice Calling*! Live, Love, Show Compassion, Be Changed—*Justice Calling* is a book for the ages!"

—John R. Lott, former head strength and speed development coordinator for the Arizona Cardinals, and NFL Strength Coach of the Year

Praise for *The Barefoot Tribe*

"*The Barefoot Tribe* is a call to rediscover Jesus and His way in a manner that will change the world—as it always has. Palmer's writing is as clear as it is compelling, and convicting in the best sense of that word. After reading his book, I have decided to take off my shoes and join the tribe."

—John Ortberg, bestselling author, *Who Is This Man?*; senior pastor, Menlo Park Presbyterian Church

"Nothing great for God happens without passion, and you can feel Palmer Chinchen's passion on every page of this rallying cry for the church. Far from the usual diatribe on the church's impairments and plights, *The Barefoot Tribe* is a call to arms toward a new kind of tribe that hears the cries of the world in everyday life and responds with passion to its hurts. The author's vision is not a church in pain but one that feels the pain of the world and salves its wounds. Chinchen changes each word of 'Here I Stand' to 'There We Go.' Painstaking and passionate, *The Barefoot Tribe* shows us how to 'Take a Hike.'"

—Leonard Sweet, bestselling author, *The Gospel According to Starbucks*; professor, Drew University, George Fox University; and chief contributor to sermons.com

"Palmer Chinchen is a prophet to our generation, and *The Barefoot Tribe* is his call to all who have ears to hear. Through fluid prose and captivating stories, Chinchen illuminates the true work of transformation and freedom for which we were all born. *The Barefoot Tribe* is as much a movement as a manifesto, drawing us back to the heart of the Christ whose name we bear. A must-read for all who would follow the Way of the Master. Bravo! May we all heed its beautiful and haunting call."

—Ted Dekker, *New York Times* bestselling author

"Palmer is a modern-day prophet. In this manifesto, he delivers an impassioned challenge to live like Jesus, love like Jesus, and to be—not just go to—the church that our Savior founded with His own blood. If you want comfort and confirmation, then don't read this book. But if you want to be confronted and stirred up, then you can't afford to pass up *The Barefoot Tribe*. Let's get back to the heart of the gospel. Let's take pieces of heaven to places of hell on earth. Let's join the tribe!"

—Preston M. Sprinkle, author, *Fight*, *Charis*, and *Erasing Hell*; director of Eternity Bible College's Boise extension site

"Palmer helped me to imagine a world where the reality of the kingdom is evident in the followers of the king. He gives examples of where he sees followers of Jesus taking up the call to live selflessly, and he gives countless practical areas for me to do so as well. He does all of this in a way that disarms me of my cynicism and hesitancy to believe in the organized institutions that looked the other way on issues of compassion and justice. This book has helped me to dream again of a day when the righteous rise up from indifference, of a movement that is truly known by love—and after reading it I feel compelled, not by guilt, but by inspiration, to get involved."

—David Zach, Remedy Drive

"I've had the pleasure of calling Palmer a friend for years and can say that he truly lives these words. His passion is authentic and contagious. This manifesto was a game changer for my wife and me. It was as if the things God was impressing on our hearts was put into words. It's a message that we needed to hear and a message that I believe all of us in the church need to hear. I've never been more excited to be a part of the Tribe!"

—Josh Havens, lead singer of The Afters

"If you care about the world we live in, desire to positively impact this world, and have a faith that guides you, *The Barefoot Tribe* is a must-read."

—Jay Feely, NFL kicker,
2014 NFL Man of the Year Nominee

"I've known Palmer for many years and have experienced first-hand that his passion for justice is genuine and infectious. In *Justice Calling*, Palmer reminds us that there is no separation between spirituality and justice. It's an inspiring and motivating call for the church to live compassionately, love generously, and put its faith into action."

—Josh Havens, lead singer of The Afters

JUSTICE CALLING

LIVE LOVE, SHOW COMPASSION, BE CHANGED

Palmer Chinchen, PhD

HOWARD BOOKS
An Imprint of Simon & Schuster, Inc.
New York   Nashville   London   Toronto   Sydney   New Delhi

H

Howard Books
An Imprint of Simon & Schuster, Inc.
1230 Avenue of the Americas
New York, NY 10020

First Howard Books trade paperback edition June 2016

HOWARD and colophon are trademarks of Simon & Schuster, Inc.

For information about special discounts for bulk purchases, please contact Simon & Schuster Special Sales at 1-866-506-1949 or business@simonandschuster.com.

The Simon & Schuster Speakers Bureau can bring authors to your live event. For more information or to book an event, contact the Simon & Schuster Speakers Bureau at 1-866-248-3049 or visit our website at www .simonspeakers.com.

Interior design by Davina Mock-Maniscalco

Manufactured in the United States of America

10   9   8   7   6   5   4   3   2   1

Library of Congress Cataloging-in-Publication Data is available.

ISBN 978-1-4767-6199-2
ISBN 978-1-4767-6200-5 (ebook)

For anyone who has ever felt *less than*.

CONTENTS

LOVE AND JUSTICE

"Take their order! What kind of order?" the deputy sheriff with the shotgun demanded.

This was the third time I had stopped to talk with the deputies holding the guns, guarding the women in the chain gang. And it wasn't going much better than the first time.

When I moved to Arizona I had heard of the sheriff's chain gangs, but I was certain it was an urban legend. Then I drove past one. I could hardly believe what I was seeing: young women chained at the ankles, in striped uniforms hoeing weeds, under the watch of shotgun-toting deputies. The entire scene was surreal.

Just because the women are prisoners does not mean they can be chained like circus animals and put on display.

This kind of disrespect and dehumanizing of any person is wrong at every level, for any reason. Being incarcerated does not rob a person of their right to dignity and respect. We are not some medieval, barbaric society. We are an educated people with a moral bearing who know deep in our soul when something is wrong, yet we allow a single bully sheriff to make a mockery of women and justice.

I couldn't just drive on by. I hung a U-turn, parked, and approached the deputy. He lowered his gun at my chest.

"Can I talk to you?" I asked.

He nodded.

"Could you give a message to your sheriff?" I asked.

"Sure."

"Please tell your sheriff that in Chandler we do not want women humiliated and put on display like this. Please tell him that in Chandler, we believe every person should be treated with dignity and respect. In Chandler, we don't want women shamed in his chain gangs."

The deputy said he would pass along my message.

A few months later, the chain gang was back, this time even closer to our church. I stopped again. Same routine, gun lowered and pointed at me as I approached.

"What do you want?" a deputy demanded.

"I'm sorry to say, I've asked your sheriff to not shame women and put them on display in Chandler."

"Well, what do you want me to do about that?" the deputy pressed.

Caught a bit off guard, I blurted, "It's time to leave now."

"And who are you?" he questioned.

"I am a pastor," I answered with all the authority I could muster.

"Okay," he mumbled amiably.

Without saying anything more to me, he turned to the women and announced, "Load up, we have to go now."

To be honest I was fairly surprised, but I felt pretty good about stopping the madness in Chandler . . . until I shared the encounter with a few friends. They said things like, "Palmer, you robbed the women of their opportunity to escape for a day from the confines of Tent City [the dusty, stifling-hot chain-link and barbed wire concentration camp where the sheriff insists on keeping his DUI prisoners]." Or, "Palmer, maybe *you* shamed the women and made them feel like we don't want them in Chandler."

Now I felt terrible! I couldn't win for losing. Prisoners' rights and prison reform are complex issues, and we need more good people at work on them. But there had to be something I could do *now* to express my desire to give these women back their dignity—no matter what they had done in the past.

That's when I decided the next time I passed the prisoners, instead of asking them to leave, I would take their orders.

And that's what I did the third time I approached the chain gang.

Lawrence, our coffee shop barista, burst into my office out of breath and blurted, "There's a chain gang down the street!" He knew my passion for ending the insanity.

"Grab your notepad and pen, Lawrence."

"Why?" he questioned.

"We're taking orders!"

We parked and approached the deputy—this time a female—with her gun pointed our way. "Are you reporters?" she questioned.

I don't think she liked the pads and pens.

"No, I'm a pastor," I said, smiling.

"What do you want with the notepads and pens?" she wondered sternly.

"We're here to take the women's orders."

"Orders! What kind of orders?"

"For lattes!" I answered with a smile. "Lawrence here is the best barista ever and he can make the girls any drink they want: vanilla latte, mocha latte, caramel macchiato latte, you name it!"

"I don't know if I can let you do that. I'll need to call headquarters."

She dialed her office on her cell phone, and as she explained our request she looked our way and started shaking her head no.

"Wait—ask them why not!" I pressed.

She asked for an explanation, then hung up. "They said you might put a weapon—a shank—in the coffee."

4

"What? I'm a pastor, I don't even know how to make a shank!"

That was it. No can do.

Before we left the deputy wondered, "Why do you want to bring lattes to the women anyway?"

"Because we want them to know that somebody cares, somebody loves them. And that they are treasured by God Himself, and He loves them too. And they are beautiful."

Why do I share this story? What was really going on there? This book is not really about prisoners' rights—at least, not in particular. It's about the motivation behind my meager coffee gesture, behind any work on immigration reform, or against human trafficking, or even to end extreme poverty: to champion the value and worth of every person. This may seem like a list of disparate issues, but they share a common root of the mighty tree of justice for all. And that root is shalom.

People of Shalom: Peace with Justice

The Hebrew idea of shalom saturates Scripture. Writers like David used the word often, "Peace [shalom] be within you."[1] We usually connect the idea of shalom with peace, but that definition of *shalom* is only half right. In its fullest context shalom means *peace with justice*.

We often hear *shalom* translated as *peace,* but the English word *peace* is inadequate for this powerful Hebrew idea of *shalom*. *Shalom* means much more than to simply have internal peace, it includes justice for all of society. Justice and shalom are tightly connected, because justice is how shalom is restored when it is absent. For example, when the Jewish people are in captivity in Babylon God tells them to "Seek the *shalom* of the city to which I have sent you."[2] In other words, they are to pursue the flourishing of the whole city, not just have internal personal peace.

I hear a lot of Christians chafe at the words *social justice*. I think they miss that social justice is most about being for the least, and no one can argue that of all the people Jesus was for, he was for the least and the last.

Unfortunately, many people now associate the term *social justice* with a political platform or political party. I invite you to undo your thinking on this and see how deeply biblical it is to meet a society's daily needs.

"Truly, I say to you," Jesus says, "as you did it to one of the least of these my brothers or sisters of mine, you did it to me."

I think we miss that as followers of Jesus—disciples—we are his means of spreading peace with justice in our neighborhoods, cities, and the world. We—you—are meant to be a blessing in the world. What do I mean by that?

The Old Testament prophet Jeremiah sent the most interesting message to God's people who lived in exile in Babylon: "Build homes, and plan to stay. Plant gardens, and eat the food they produce. Marry and have children. Then find spouses for them so that you may have many grandchildren. Multiply!"[3]

So God says bless the city you live in. Do not remain separated and segregated.

The Jewish captives in Babylon were mostly from Jerusalem. In Hebrew, *Jerusalem* comes from two words, *Ir* and *shalem*. *Ir* means city, *shalem* comes from shalom, which means "peace with justice." So the very name of their prized holy city, Jerusalem, means "city of peace with justice." Isn't that beautiful?

Through the prophet Jeremiah, God is asking the Jews from the "city of peace with justice" to actively work for the shalom of their city of exile, Babylon. It's as if God sent them to bring shalom to a new city. The message is the same for us in our city, in our neighborhoods, in our country, and in our world.

People of Peace with Justice Hear Their Neighbors

When the signs that read Black Lives Matter and No Justice, No Peace filled the suburban streets of a large midwestern city, I called a longtime friend who lives in a neighboring community to ask, "So, have you been out on the streets to walk with the people who are marching?"

"No," he said, laughing. "I haven't thought much about that."

"Have the pastors from your church been there? What did they say on Sunday morning?" I know the church well, with its redbrick facade, white columns and steeple, and polished cars filling the parking lot out front.

"No, they haven't been there, either, and no, they have not said anything from the pulpit," he answered soberly.

Do you see the irony? Do you see the inconsistency? In the same city, people in one neighborhood walk the streets holding signs overhead reading No Justice, No Peace, while in another, people gather to sing songs about Jesus, read Bible verses about God, and pray prayers—without saying a word about the oppression of a people in the neighborhood next door.

The silence is deafening.

The absence of words on justice in our worship is glaring.

I don't say this to judge one church and its pastors. I say this because the silence is epidemic.

Recently, when a New Yorker named Eric Garner cried

out, "I can't breathe," no one seemed to listen. He died because his cries fell on deaf ears.

Today, entire communities are crying out, *I can't breathe.* My question is, are the people of God listening? When we fail to hear our neighbors, we have a problem.

At the root of the problem is our separation of spirituality from justice. In the church today, we tend to view these concepts as belonging in two separate arenas. Most consider "doing justice" as a nice thing to tack on to our spirituality, a kind of afterthought to our spiritual formation—or else a pernicious proof of "works-based salvation."

For the most part we have made spiritual formation about personal piety a gospel of morality. If I don't smoke, don't drink too much, don't curse, and don't watch *South Park,* then I'm doing pretty good at being a Christian.

That is not even close to what following God is truly about.

When the ancients of Scripture spoke clearly of *authentic spirituality,* they saw no separation between spirituality and justice:

Solomon—*Speak up for the poor and helpless, and see that they get justice.*[4]

Isaiah—*Break the chains of injustice . . . set the oppressed free.*[5]

Micah—*Do justice, love mercy.*[6]

Amos—*Let justice roll like a river.*[7]

Jesus Christ—*He has sent me to proclaim freedom for prisoners and . . . set the oppressed free.*[8]

I believe what is missing in our spirituality today is a passion for justice, a deep desire to see the world made right—as good and beautiful as God intended. I believe what is needed most in the personal lives of Christians and in our churches today is a turn toward justice.

This book is a call for a *justice conversion* in the church.

We talk a great deal of the need for a *personal conversion*, a right apologetic, but that language implies a kind of intellectual transaction with God. It stops short of us becoming the kind of people God calls us to be to a broken world. The great need today is a *justice conversion*.

We need a confession and conversion away from our spiteful attitudes toward immigrants and the poor and our racial stereotypes—toward a spirituality drenched with compassion and love for all.

In this book, I want to explore what it looks like for the people of God truly to live together in shalom—peace with justice. I want to explore what justice has to do with our sense of *purpose*, our deep longing for *authenticity* as humans and as followers of Christ, and our *mission* of justice in this world. Issues of injustice break the heart of God and should break ours. Because maybe love and justice, and the way we live every day, is our finest apologetic—the best proof of authentic spirituality of all.

Chapter 1

WHY SOCIAL JUSTICE MATTERS

"**S**top using that phrase *social justice* when you preach," the man steamed. I couldn't believe what I was hearing. He was a church leader, and he wanted to silence me on justice? The trouble is, I'm a bit of a rebel. So all his bad attitude did was make me read a pile of Scripture on the next Sunday that demands we be people of justice.

This man wasn't alone, though. When I speak on college campuses, at Christian conferences, or in churches, I know the one phrase that always makes people squirm uncomfortably in their seats is *social justice*.

People don't seem to mind the word *justice*. It's the *social* part that vexes them. That's a bit odd, because when the

11

prophets like Amos or Isaiah or Moses—or Jesus Himself—talked about justice, it was always social.

Why do some flinch at the word, I wonder? Is it because we might actually have to do something tangible with our spirituality? Is it because we must speak up for or defend a population that we have been conditioned to be biased against? Is it because a political party or a news channel has told us this is an evil thing? Is it greed, because we might have to share what we have with the poor or the immigrant?

I wonder.

The Christian community stands divided on the issue of spirituality and justice. Large camps of evangelicals have dug their heels into the ground on one side to say our gospel is not about social justice. On the other side of the line stand those who reject a gospel sans justice and demand options for the poor, a response to oppression, and a spirituality that embraces mercy.

Does social justice matter? Is it critical to the life and growth of God's people after all? The answer from the Bible is clear: God is disturbed by injustice, He wants it stopped, and you are His plan for making things the way they're supposed to be.

At the root of understanding the *why* of social justice are three foundational principles: the image of God, the common good, and the good news of Jesus.

Image of God

When we understand the idea of the *imago Dei,* the image of God, as spoken from the opening lines of the garden story, we begin to understand justice.

The concept of *imago Dei* presented in Genesis makes clear that all people, for all time, have innate value, worth, and beauty, because all people are made in the image of God. Some act as though this is a theological identity limited to those who call themselves Christians. It's not. The *imago Dei* resides in every person who walks planet earth. And because of this, every person has innate value and is worthy of equal dignity and respect—regardless of race, gender, wealth, ethnicity, immigration status, background, or any other factor.

Common Good

Social justice is a reclaiming of God's original intent for humankind: to make the world a place where basic needs are met, people thrive, and there is shalom—peace with justice. One of our great godly responsibilities on earth is the *remaking and healing* of society so that all people—especially the disadvantaged and marginalized—can flourish.

To do this, we must identify the root causes of poverty,

hunger, and oppression; then give our lives—our best abilities and resources—to changing those structures and practices that create discrimination and hunger, for example.

Tribal people understand the common good and the power of collaboration. Liberians where I grew up say, "Three rocks can cook rice." In other words, you cannot balance a pot over a fire on one rock or even two rocks; you need three rocks to hold the pot. They say this because everything in the village requires collaboration by the tribe. When rice is planted, one person does not plant the rice; not even two. When it's time to plant, the entire village comes to your farm to hoe and scatter seed. Because they know when the time comes to plant their farm, you will be there, too.

No one in the village plants alone, repairs their roof alone, or makes mud bricks alone—or cries alone.

The tension facing the church as we know it is that we have privatized our faith. Knowing God, for example, has become a *personal decision*. And sometimes we talk about *personal quiet times* as the pinnacle of spirituality. The problem is, when Jesus lays out this great command, He explains that the best form of spirituality is to care for your neighbor. All the inner pursuit of good is not the best we can do: pursuing good for all is.

In his brilliant voice in the conversation on justice, Walter Brueggemann describes the Christian dispassion toward the common good as "the great crisis among us."[1]

He explains how the disadvantaged live in a state of anxiety, without justice, without peace.

Social Justice Is Good News

My experience is, when church people talk about the gospel they infer a message that is preached—something to be spoken. And the evangelical has been very good at this for the past fifty years.

The trouble is, this is not the only way Jesus talked about good news. When we read His words in Matthew or Luke, we realize the gospel includes a clear *doing* component: feed the hungry, end the oppression. So when Christians remain silent on issues of injustice, we minimize the good news as Jesus presented it.

When Jesus talked about good news, it always included a social component—of justice, healing, equality, and love. When we present a gospel as something that is only for our mind and heart, we halve the gospel. We truncate it, and very often we make it something so ethereal it never changes the world we live in.

I invite you to expand your idea of "good news" and see the whole gospel—something we speak as well as something we must do. The good news of Jesus includes social justice; there is simply no getting around that. You would have to tear pages out of your Bible to miss this.

Today I see more and more Christ followers realizing the biblical value of social justice and how living out Jesus' commands to love the least and last, share with the poor, and care for sick are actually clearer and often the best presentation of the good news.

Sometimes I hear people say doing justice is a nice thing to do *after we preach.* Or, social justice is a nice way to attract people to the gospel. But that's just manipulation—cheap marketing of sorts. And it misses the point. Social justice is much deeper than an add-on or a marketing ploy. It's to be an intrinsic part of our identity in Christ.

You cannot separate Jesus from justice. Read the miracle stories of the Gospels. Notice that Jesus never healed or gave dignity in order to trick someone into believing. Rather, someone was desperate, so He met the need.

Following Christ requires a life intertwined with social justice. If we fail to *do* the good news—end prejudice, embrace the immigrant, for example—then we are simply not living the Jesus kind of life.

The Long Story of Christian Social Justice

The story of social justice is long, stretching for centuries. The impression of some seems to be that social justice is either a nouveau trend of the next generation or a remnant of mid-twentieth-century liberal theology.

Not so. The story begins before Jesus, with ancient prophets like Amos, Isaiah, and Micah calling for justice and compassion for the poor. Jesus, who fulfilled the law, and the prophets took up the same call. Then, two thousand years ago, the first church shared all they had with each other and with the poor.

By the third century, Christianity was spreading wildly through the Roman Empire; so did the reputation of Christians as being the saviors of babies. At the time, Romans and pagans of all ethnicities widely practiced *exposure*, the abandoning of unwanted infants. Infanticide was an acceptable option for the poor, who could not afford an extra mouth to feed; for the Romans, who prized boys and discarded unwanted baby girls; and for any parents with a child born with a deformity. Christians were different. Because Jesus loved children, they valued the infant and regularly rescued abandoned babies. The homes of Christians turned into safe havens, and the first monasteries become sanctuaries for unwanted babies and children.

Of course every child has heard of St. Nicholas, but what most do not know is that he was actually a third-century historical figure—often described as the first abolitionist. Nicholas served as the bishop of Myra, in present-day Turkey, and was widely known for being passionate about charity and social justice, caring for the neglected in his community, and being the protector of children.

A story is told of one poor man with three daughters.

The man would never have the required dowries for his daughters to marry, so they would certainly be sold into slavery. The story goes that St. Nicholas tossed a bag of gold through an open window into the poor man's house, enough money to save each girl from slavery. One bag landed in a stocking drying by the fire . . . of course.

Much more recently, in the mid-nineteenth century, when the American South was plagued by slavery, dozens of churches from Savannah to Detroit helped form the Underground Railroad, which carried slaves to freedom. This critical social justice movement—fueled primarily by Christians and churches—became a key factor in ending slavery.

Compassion and generosity were prominent values among every early American denomination, Presbyterians, Congregationalists, and Anglicans alike. The popular eighteenth-century founder of the Methodist movement, John Wesley, famously instructed, "Put yourself in the place of every poor man and deal with him as you would God deal with you." As a result of his influence Methodists became leaders in many social issues of the day, including prison reform and abolishing slavery.

My point is, in years past the church actually led the way on social justice issues. However, in the 1920s a disconnect grew when the modern evangelical movement began to swell. In reaction to the "liberals," who were building hospitals and schools, some chose a "personal" gospel over a Jesus kind of gospel.

The focus turned highly individualistic: "I have *my personal* quiet time." The emphasis was on being saved from hell and making it into heaven after we die. The entire salvation process was internal, personal, transcendent, of the *heart* and *soul*, to the exclusion of the world around.

Growing up, I heard that caring for people's basic needs was for the Catholics and liberals. Ironically, evangelicals are known for our reverence of the Bible, but we seem to have missed the parts of the Bible on which the theology of social justice is based. Like the part when Jesus' brother James says, "How can you show me your faith if you don't have good deeds? I will show you my faith by my good deeds."[2]

Where we need to begin our gospel conversation is with Jesus, because Jesus was the embodiment of good news and His life was its best demonstration. He kept saying *follow My example*. And we must.

Justice Conversion

I have my own justice conversion story.

I was raised an evangelical. We attended seminars, memorized the laws, and taught classes on evangelism. That's what we did. Please don't misunderstand me; these were all good things, but evangelism seemed to be the extent of our Christian duty.

We also talked about being *deep*. The word was elusive and intangible. People would sometimes say their pastor's teaching was not deep enough for them so they were going somewhere else. I think that's the most hurtful stone Christians hurl at their pastor, because the accusation is so subjective—and personal. I soon realized people threw that stone because they just wanted to hurt you, not because they aspired to something spiritual. But the jabs caused me to work hard to be deeper in my relationship with God, even though no one was quite sure what that meant or when we had arrived.

And then I moved to the poorest nation on earth, Malawi, with my wife, Veronica, and our four sons, where I taught at African Bible College.

While living in Malawi, for the first time in my life, I saw grown men walk the streets of the capital city in tattered, threadbare suit jackets, pants worn through to the bare knee—but washed and pressed neat with a charcoal iron—and barefoot. I had never before seen grown men in a city walk barefoot.

My friend Moses had twin daughters, both of whom died at three months old from malaria. My wife and I had to sit with another young friend to tell her the AIDS test was positive. On one afternoon I drove to three different hospitals—using the term in its most generous sense—looking for an X-ray machine that worked to take images of my friend Christopher's compound fracture. I helped pull the dead body of a man from a swamp who drowned when he had an epileptic seizure—something for which in America we have a dozen different medications.

I had seen enough. Something started to bother me. Why are churches and missionaries all over this country building churches, evangelizing, and holding outreach crusades, but doing practically nothing to end the poverty or stop the pandemics?

What kind of good news is this, if we plant churches and train pastors to preach on Sunday but never do anything about the barefoot man on the street on Monday?

I wrote curriculum for a course I titled "A Theology of Suffering." Halfway through the semester it hit me: the poor do not have to remain poor. That was never Jesus'— let alone God's—intention. I had heard Jesus' words twisted by preachers who said, "The poor will always be among us."[3] Implying, ignore them because the whole thing is hopeless. It's not. Jesus was talking to Judas about a specific issue. This was not an inescapable destiny. There is hope.

With my class of Malawian college students we read Shūsako Endō's riveting novel *Silence,* Brennan Manning's *Ragamuffin Gospel,* and Henri Nouwen's *The Wounded Healer.* I saw in all of these Jesus' passion for the least and the last and the trampled down, and I saw my own apathy. That semester something happened to me at the soul level. I realized I, too, had been silent about the injustice and oppression. It hurt my heart, and it changed me. I know now that this was my *justice conversion*.

Where Do the Fires of Injustice Still Burn?

Dark plumes of smoke rose ominously over South Central Los Angeles. The riots raged just thirteen miles from our suburban home, from our church.

A video camera had recorded the violent, senseless beating of an African American man named Rodney King by the LAPD. The neighbors and neighborhoods had had *enough*.

The protests and riots continued for a week. The National Guard, the infantry, and the 1st Marine Division were all called in—and at church we said nothing. We did nothing.

I wish we had. I wish *I* had. I was only a youth pastor, but I had a voice. I should have spoken up. But that's not what nice church people in the suburbs did. We stayed silent and separated from the blighted neighborhoods and the inner-city slums—and people of the "other" race.

It took me fifteen more years to find the courage to begin saying the things the Bible tells us to say. I regret it took so long, because those kinds of fires still burn and our kind of church people are still silent. It's time for all of us to say *enough*.

Not long ago, in a Dhaka, Bangladesh, clothing factory, people burned to death inside. More than a thousand garment workers were working furiously to fill orders when alarm bells sounded. As black smoke swallowed the building and workers ran for the exits, their managers told them to get back to work. There were no sprinklers or fire escapes. Within minutes, the entire factory was engulfed in flames, and kept burning for seventeen hours.[4]

When the fire finally stopped, singed Walmart and Disney logos littered the rubble. That's whose orders the garment workers were putting in sixteen-hour days to fill. Issues of injustice litter our country and the globe like the multinational conglomerates' charred logos. The root of the issue is that too many of us consumers consume without a conscience. We like our stuff and we want it cheap. When we are careless with our wants, the poor suffer.

Some injustice gets close and personal and makes you burn on the inside, like when my friend Alex was stopped because of the color of his skin.

Alex—on our church staff—was on his way to work when he noticed a sheriff's deputy following him. After about a mile, the deputy pulled up next to him, looked through his window, and turned on his lights. Rather than ask Alex for his license and registration, he demanded, "Show me your proof of residency."

Alex tried to hand the officer his driver's license and registration, but the officer barked angrily, "I said *proof of residency.*"

You see, Alex is Hispanic. That's why the officer asked for his "proof of residency." But what is that anyway? Do we have a national ID card I don't know about? Are we all supposed to carry our birth certificate or passport? When did this happen?

We do this in our county now, we harass people because of their skin color. When will we decide to stop?

We seem to have forgotten that Jesus was *for* the immigrant. He shocked the religious establishment of His day by embracing the immigrant, like the foreign woman He asked for a drink in Sychar. He championed immigrants as righteous heroes in His stories, like the compassionate Samaritan. And He said things like, "I was a foreigner and you invited Me in."

The brilliant global economist Jeffrey Sachs says we really can extinguish the fire of extreme poverty—we just need more hoses.[5] Sachs is adamant that absolute poverty—people living on less than two dollars a day—can be ended in the next ten years. The key is for our efforts to be collaborative, massive, and concentrated. Then the desperate poor can be set free from their poverty trap.

The question is, what will you do? A few hoses, Sachs says, is not enough. But when we have thousands of advocates, thousands of voices, thousands of people giving their best thinking and efforts to find innovate solutions to the world's most vexing social problems—like extreme poverty—we can put the fires out.

This book is about a way forward, an offer of the hand of accord to each of us, on either side of the debate. A way to end the dispassion and live deeply spiritual lives that promote biblical, social justice for all people.

In *Justice Calling* we will examine the infinite connection between spirituality and justice. We will see how a life dedicated to ending the oppression, giving dignity and hope to the marginalized, being a voice for the silenced, and spreading the love of God among those who feel trampled by society leads not only to the world God is calling us to help remake, but also to the most deeply spiritual life we can have.

Today a revolution for justice is surging through the streets of our society. When the history books are written, when your grandchildren speak of this day, where will you have been? What will they say about you? Will you be on the side of God himself, speaking up for the marginalized, defending the immigrant poor, walking the blighted neighborhood streets in solidarity? Or will you sit sleepy on your sofa, nodding your approval of the skeptics and critics? *Justice Calling* is your invitation to get up off the sofa, step outside, and walk the streets Jesus walked when He was here on earth.

Chapter 2

CARRY ME HALFWAY

Growing up in the Liberian jungle, I found a lot to fear: the five-step mamba, the crocodile, malaria, and the army ants that eat you when you sleep—to name a few. But of all the evil things I feared, I feared the Heartman the most. His job was to bring back a human sacrifice for the witch doctor. My Liberian friends always warned us to be careful at night, because the Heartman was looking for children. He carried a machete and a gunnysack and always wore white.

I might still doubt the existence of the Heartman, if the Heartman hadn't chased me—along with my twin brother, Paul, and my friends Wolo, Seeku, Tall, and Klebo—one moonless rainy-season night.

The drizzle made the path muddy when we started the

walk back to our house in the dark from Sunday-night chapel. My parents stayed after the service, visiting, but Paul and I wanted to get home. So we asked Wolo and Thomas to walk with us, to "carry us halfway." The heavy clouds, with the drizzling rain, made the night dark as a crypt. We didn't have a flashlight or lantern, but we had Thomas Kleebo. And Thomas was from the bush. He could see way into the night.

We talked quietly as we walked the length of the grass airfield, from one end of the mission to the other. The stretch between had no homes, no dorms, no people—just the swamp with palm nut trees, snakes, and crocs. As we passed the swamp where the path led to Plandabalebo, the village of the witch doctor, Thomas froze and hissed under his breath, "Look. Somebody's there!"

I strained my eyes to see into the foggy silhouette of palm nut trees in the swamp. "I don't see anything," I whispered back hopefully.

"Man is there! Look good."

Then I saw him, white trousers, white shirt, and no flashlight. Liberian men, even deep in the bush, never walk without a flashlight or lantern. And nobody wears white at night, because people will accuse you of doing witchcraft or being a spirit. Except the Heartman.

Then, at once it seemed, all of us saw him.

No one yelled, "Run!" No one needed to. No one shouted anything. We just ran, ran for all we were worth. We ran like the water deer run in the night. We didn't stop running. We didn't look back until we burst through the front door of our yellow house in the bush and slammed it shut.

That's why Liberians say, "Carry me halfway."

When the African sun dims and slowly fades into the dark jungle canopy and it's time to head home, Liberians always turn to their friends and quietly ask, "Carry me halfway."

The request is relationally loaded. What they are really saying is:

The walk home will be so much sweeter with a friend.

And the truth is, it's getting dark and I feel afraid.

Come walk with me.

I don't want to walk alone.

So a crowd of friends gathers to walk you home. But never just halfway—they say "halfway" only to be polite—they always walk you all the way home.

And that is what I hope to do with you in *Justice Calling*.

The church does well carrying people halfway—spiritually. But for some reason, we seem to stop there, in the darkness, with the lights of home just barely visible in the distance.

We live spiritually underdeveloped and are unaware of our own condition. Like infants trapped in adult bodies, we feed on milk, Paul in the Bible says, never nearing our full potential.

Something is strangely missing.

Because you were created for more.

A life brimming with purpose, authenticity, and justice.

Stuck Halfway

"She said no one's crossing the border, it's not safe!" one of our doctors explained the moment I arrived in Barahona, Dominican Republic. He said that was the announcement from the self-appointed disaster response team head of the nonprofit we had come to serve with in the DR just after the devastating earthquake in Haiti.

"Why in the world are you up there unloading a truck?" I yelled at Paul, our team leader, perched high on a pile of boxes with members of our medical team.

"The truck was loaded with food for orphanages in Haiti, but the American lady said to unload it, it's not going," Paul shouted back.

I was so confused.

Days after the earthquake we had sent a team of ten doctors and nurses from our church to respond to the crisis; three days later I flew down to join them. For three days they had cared for Haitian children with crush fractures. Initially, our team was the only medical help on the ground. Now there were more than fifty medical personal caring for eleven children. It was time to continue across the border where thousands more were desperate for help.

"Are you serious?" I asked our doctors and nurses.

"Yes, the doctor in charge is saying it's not safe in Haiti, so no one is allowed to cross the border."

Still skeptical of a disaster response team not being allowed to reach the disaster, I joined a meeting called by the doctor in charge.

It became clear that this was her first time in a developing country and her first time responding to a disaster. She stood up and talked about all the dangers and uncertainty in Haiti. "We unloaded the truck and kept it from going because we believe bandits will jump on it to loot it and shoot the driver. The reservoir near the border is unstable and could flood the road any moment. Also, if doctors and nurses go into Haiti, they could be taken hostage and held for ransom by the gangs of Cité Soleil. A lot of bad things are happening in Haiti. So we are going to stay here, where it is safe. And no one, I repeat, no one is going to Haiti."

I sat there thinking, *This is ludicrous.* To be fair, this aid worker was there, where many others were not. She was new to the situation and new to the responsibility. And I suppose she was doing her best to grapple with the conflicting desires to do good and keep people safe. But the real desperation was *on the other half of the island.* Our team had traveled thousands of miles to care for desperate people but we were only halfway there.

That's when I got up and slipped out. As her meeting continued, I called our team together.

"We leave at 6 a.m."

"What?" someone in our group asked. "The American lady just said no one is allowed to cross the border."

My answer went something like, "Yeah, I heard that, too. But, A, the kids here now have incredible round-the-clock care, and at this point all of you are desperately needed in Haiti. B, I don't work for this NGO (she's not the boss of me). And, C, I rented my own Durango.

"Each of you has something God needs you to do in Haiti," I continued. "You've done a superb job in the DR, but you're just halfway. Now it's time to go all the way to Port-au-Prince."

We left at first light.

Is There More?

The longing to grow and thrive sits deep in every human soul.

Why do we always ask parents of newborns, "How much do they weigh?" Because we know the infant will only be healthy if it's growing chubbier by the day. Growth matters.

My cousin Ralph thinks he's funny. Whenever I used to see him at family gatherings like Thanksgiving or Christmas, when I was in high school, he would look at my twin brother and me with feigned disbelief and say, "You look smaller!" He knew that drove us mad because we always wanted to be bigger.

Al from Canada lived across the hall from me at Biola University and religiously lifted weights. Every morning when I walked by his room he had a tape measure wrapped around his bicep. But whenever Jim—next room over—saw Al checking the size of his arms, he would exclaim, "Al, you look smaller today!" For some reason Al believed him, and he would sputter, "Really, I look smaller?" Jim was making Al nuts.

We all want to "grow." We all want to "be stronger" and "mature." There's something innate in the human soul that longs for this. Most Christians want to be that deep, mature follower of Christ, but for some reason we just can't seem to find our way there. We're not quite sure how it happens. Is it by memorizing more Bible verses? Should we read more thick books by theologians? Will a small group that asks stinging questions about our thought life do it? If I hold my hands up during worship, am I a deeper person? Nobody seems very sure. So we all just "act" spiritual, while depth remains an elusive facade.

I wrote this book because I believe there is a way to a faith that is deep, ferocious, and full of life.

The Rest of the Discipleship

Be a disciple. Make disciples. We've known that for years. But what does it mean to actually be the kind of disciple Jesus wanted?

Mark the disciple records this intriguing interaction between Jesus and a Hebrew theologian who asked what is the most important aspect of the human life. Jesus says, "Love God. Love others." And the theologian gets it, because most Jews were busy offering all kinds of sacrifices, busy with all kinds of religious things—while ignoring their neighbors. We seem to be doing the same.

Out of college I became a student ministry pastor and taught discipleship, led discipleship groups, and asked people to disciple me. Did this for years—never really sure when I or anyone else would finish learning to be a disciple. It seemed to be a course with no graduation date.

From the best I could tell, being a disciple was primarily something that happened in our heads and in our "heart," in the most personal and introspective way. We were never made to believe that meeting the needs of the other was part of being a disciple. None of the spiritual growth charts or circular models of discipleship ever included stopping injustice and ending oppression as part of the process.

Maybe this is why I like James Bryant Smith's (*The Good and Beautiful Life*) word *apprentice* when he speaks of being followers of Christ. Smith says we are apprentices of Jesus, and expected to *do* the things Jesus did.

Because when Jesus paints the picture of apprenticeship it looks different. It's actually rather straightforward: love God, love others, and go help others do the same.[1]

To overlook this fuller picture is to risk being only half the person God made you to be.

Spiritual Development

Developmental theory has been a part of educational studies for decades. But only recently has developmental theory been applied to Christian education and spiritual growth. Efforts to integrate developmental theory with spiritual growth can be traced to Horace Bushnell, a nineteenth-century theologian who wrote widely on spiritual nurture, but more recently, the work of Emory University theologian and spiritual formation thinker James Fowler has drawn the most attention.

Using Swiss development psychologist and philosopher Jean Piaget's model of cognitive development and Lawrence Kohlberg's theory of moral development as a framework, Fowler developed a taxonomy of *teleios* (spiritual maturity). That is, a way of explaining what it looks like to progress from an early grasp of faith to a fully formed, world-changing faith. His concept includes six stages, which I will paraphrase and summarize here:

> *Primary faith* describes childlike faith when beliefs are shaped by biblical stories, with a basic understanding of theology.

Literal faith is the stage at which a more logical and coherent understating of faith emerges.

Relational faith comes when a person begins to identify as a follower of Christ through the strong relationships they form in the Christian community.

Passionate faith describes the stage when personal ownership is taken of what one believes, and the longing for a God-given purpose emerges.

Authentic faith brings a new willingness to cherish paradox and the apparent contradictions of differing perspectives, as well as increased tolerance and grace toward others.

The final stage, *collective faith*, is marked by the beauty of selfless living, when a person becomes far more concerned with justice and the common good than self-preservation and personal piety.

I find Fowler's stages of faith to be an intriguing point of reference in the justice conversation. This book is not an academic study on faith stages, nor does it do more than scratch the surface on Fowler's work. But taking it as meaningful grounding, I'll explore ways in which we grow toward complete *teleios* by focusing on the final three stages of development.

Christians have been good at reaching the first three

phases: *primary* faith, *literal* faith, and *relational* faith. But if we stop there, we only get halfway. In this book, we're going to look at the second half of spiritual development, the last three phases: *passionate* faith (living with purpose), *authentic* faith, and *collective* or missional faith.

I hope you crave more, because as the Jesus apprentice Peter writes, "then you'll grow up mature."[2]

Stuck Halfway

Connecting social justice to spiritual growth is not just Fowler's idea or my idea. An army of other Christian thinkers agree.

Renowned author and pastor Tim Keller (*Generous Justice*), for example, writes about the Hebrew idea of *tzadeqah*. The word is usually translated as "being righteous." What can be missed is that it refers to a life of right relationships.

When most Christians hear the word *righteous,* they think of it as an issue of personal moral virtue, and having more personal quiet time, prayer, and memorizing Bible verses. Keller says if we think this way, we miss what righteousness in the Bible is really about: "In the Bible, *tzadeqah* refers to day-to-day living in which a person conducts all relationships in family and society with fairness, generosity and equity . . . *tzadeqah* is primarily about being in a right relationship with God, the righteous life that results is profoundly social."[3]

Do you see how if we make the gospel only about our personal morality it is lacking, going only halfway?

Humanitarian Richard Stearns writes about the "halfway" gospel, too: "There is a real problem with this limited view of the kingdom of God; it is not the whole gospel. Instead, it's a gospel with a gaping hole." He explains that when we focus only on telling others what to believe, we have reduced the gospel to half of what God planned. "Our charge is to both proclaim and embody the gospel so they can see, hear, and feel God's love in tangible ways."[4]

The contemplative Christian author Henri Nouwen always connected spiritual formation with being people of healing. He used the compelling metaphor of Jesus as *the wounded healer* "who will free us from hatred and oppression, from racism and war—a messiah who will let peace and justice take their rightful place." Like Jesus, he says, we in turn are called to be wounded healers to the weak, broken, sick, poor, lonely, forgotten, anxious, and lost.[5]

Justice revolutionary Shane Claiborne is adamant about Christians sharing the whole gospel, not just half. "Come and see. Let me show you Jesus with skin on," he says. "Sometimes we have evangelicals (usually from the suburbs) ask how we 'evangelize' people.'" He tells them, "We are trying to shout the gospel with our lives."[6]

The issue at stake is our relationship with God. Spiritual

formation is not simply about improving yourself. Spiritual growth is ultimately about your relationship with God Himself. Justice is the muscle we exercise to make the relationship stronger. The more your heart beats for justice, the more it beats in rhythm with the heart of God. Conversely, if we neglect justice, then we progressively drift further from intimacy with Him.

Let's say a woman marries a man who says he loves her. But soon she starts to notice that he says, "I love you," a lot, but he rarely shows it. He lies on the sofa watching TV while she fixes dinner, eats it quickly during commercials, then resumes the position as she does the dishes. He throws his dirty socks on the floor, ignores the full garbage cans, and leaves the toilet seat up. Finally one night she bursts out in tears: "Don't you love me?"

With all sincerity, he answers, "Sure I do. I think about how much I love you all the time. I feel love for you deep in my heart. I even tell people at work how much I love you."

Her response? "Then show it!"

Justice is God's love language. He says, "I, the Lord, love justice."[7]

You see, connecting social justice with spiritual formation is *God's* idea. We somehow forget the entire narrative arc of Scripture is God's redemption of peoples and nations. The flourishing was never personal, let alone limited to an internal esoteric experience; it was always a thriving of the entire community, and it included their land and their homes.

When Jesus' mother, Mary, bares her soul, she sings a reminder that God's redemptive work spans centuries and continents. It is no limited personal thing:

> He knocked tyrants off their high horses,
> pulled victims out of the mud.
> The starving poor sat down to a banquet;
> the callous rich were left out in the cold.
> He embraced his chosen child, Israel;
> he remembered and piled on the mercies, piled them
>   high.
> It's exactly what he promised,
> beginning with Abraham and right up to now.[8]

Perhaps the most graphic illustration of the critical connection between spirituality and justice comes from Jesus Himself, when He tells the story of a rich man and the homeless man outside his gated community.[9]

The moneyed man in the fancy clothes walks past the diseased, destitute man day after day, ignoring his most basic, obvious needs: food, water, clothes, a place to sleep. As a result, Jesus says, the leisure-class man ends up in hell.

When we read Jesus' words and think about His acts, how can we separate social justice from spiritual formation?

In examining Fowler's model (or using other, similar

models), you might assume that most Christians do reach the upper stages of faith. Wrong. Not even close. Fowler, along with contemporary educators and theologians like Perry Downs, Linda Cannell, and Ted Ward, widely agree that most Christians stop maturing at stage three—halfway.

People begin attending church and find comfort in the community, but then become stuck in the routine of tradition and simply stop growing, like a bonsai tree in a pot.

But I believe there is a way forward, into the upper stages—a way toward deeper spirituality, greater purpose, and a flourishing life.

The Upper Stage

One of the most dramatic fixtures of Elizabethan theaters was the upper stage. The main stage, or lower stage, was of course where most of the drama played. But in Shakespearean plays, for example, the most dramatic, powerful scenes were reserved for the upper stage. And the upper stage was best viewed from prized upper box seats, to which only a few privileged spectators had access.

So the lower stage was wide and broad, and everyone could enjoy. But the upper stage was much smaller, and only a few would get to experience the complete story.

The more I read, the more I dive in, the more I understand spiritual development, the more clear it becomes that what is missing in the lives of so many are the three critical aspects of spirituality. These aspects move us through the upper stages of spiritual formation: *purpose, authenticity,* and *justice.* These three strands draw together to pull us toward one overarching goal: to move us up the path of spiritual maturation—in a single word, *flourish.*

These three critical components describe the final three upper stages of faith:

The quest for *purpose.*
The longing for *authenticity.*
The passion for *justice.*

These three strands not only represent the upper stages of Fowler's faith-stage model, they also represent the three cries of the future church. The next-generation Christian longs for *purpose*: "Why am I here?" They demand *authenticity*: "Don't sell us cheap imitations." And they want *justice*: "We are for the common good and against oppression."

The church of previous generations did not always champion these values. Today, however, if you and your church have aspirations of reaching and growing mature followers of Christ, these three values—*purpose, authenticity,* and *justice*—must become central to your life and ministry.

If we are okay with halfway, than we never reach the top of Bellevue la Montagne, "the mountain called Beautiful." The mountain that rises up from the sea as a dramatic cyclorama to Port-au-Prince.

Back to the D.R. border: With the sun rising over the Sierra de Baoruco—mountains that separate the Dominican Republic from Haiti—we drove toward the Haitian border. The customs post was sheer chaos, with maddening crowds trying to reach their desperate families in Port-au-Prince. We paid a few immigration fees and finally just drove around the back of the border post, past the mobs and into Haiti. Our first stop was just five minutes into the country at a field hospital; literally, patients lying on mattresses in a field—practically every patient had an amputation or crush fracture. Our doctors met their doctors, who ecstatically accepted the help and the boxes of Percocet we brought from our church in Arizona. "We've run out of painkillers," they explained, "and we've been performing amputations with Tylenol!"

We continued on to Port-au-Prince, following an American radio Bible teacher who said the orphanage his station sponsored was damaged beyond repair by the earthquake and would love our help.

We found about thirty orphans huddled in the front yard of a home, where they also slept at night. The orphanage director, Johnny, pleaded for us to return with the food the American woman had made us unload from the truck: "We ran out of food five days ago. The neighbors have been sharing what they have with the children."

"I'll be back with a truckload of food tomorrow," I promised Johnny—even if I had to load it myself in the dark of night.

We came back the next day with the truck filled with more food than they kids could eat in a month. An American preacher in camouflage army fatigues fell out of a tree, trying to hang a blue tarp over where the kids slept at night. The Haitian helping him was stung by a wasp.

"Johnny, how long are the kids going to sleep on the grass and dirt under the blue tarp in front of this house?" I asked.

"Well, the preacher promised to come next week and put up a tent for the kids."

"The kids need something more permanent than a tent," I said. "If you would like, I will come back in thirty days with a crew to build a dorm for the kids."

"Of course!" Johnny answered. He sounded excited, but skeptical.

A month later we were back, this time with twenty-two construction workers. The dorm went up in seven days.

My good friend Ben Greene took me up Bellevue la Montagne. He said practically every home on the mountain had collapsed in the earthquake. He wanted me to meet a pastor whose church and home had crumbled.

The drive up was painstakingly slow and rugged. We pulled up to where the pastor's home and church once stood, only to be told he and his wife were mourning the death of their toddler, who had died just hours earlier.

In spite of the tragedy, the pastor came out from his tin shelter to greet us. His name was Pastor Felix. He didn't seem to want to talk much of his son or his home. He kept telling me—a pastor, too—about his lost church. "Will you help me rebuild it, Pastor Palmer?" he pleaded with desperation in his voice.

I try not to make promises I can't keep, so the best I could give him was, "I will try."

We've returned half a dozen times since then to the top of the mountain called Beautiful, first to rebuild Felix's home, then his church, now his community. And we've continued returning to help Johnny build a new orphanage, start a school, and even give orphans new homes with families at our church in Arizona.

I've often thought about what would have happened if we had stopped halfway to Haiti—and not just to the people of Haiti.

If we had stopped halfway, not only would the people of Haiti have gone unaided in their greatest moment of desperation, but our people would have lost. Because our lives, our spirits would have remain unchanged.

Jeff Delp demonstrates this principle well.

I ran into Jeff this morning in our church's coffee shop as he was restocking his display of necklaces and bracelets. He laughed when he showed me his cuts and abrasions from bending nails to make the jewelry—because Jeff is not a jewelry maker. Jeff's a junior high school principal. After his initial trip to Haiti to help rebuild Pastor Felix's church, he keeps going back to train teachers who teach orphans. And while Jeff is in America, he sells handcrafted jewelry to subsidize the pay of the teachers who teach orphans, so they can feed their families.

Jeff writes on his blog about how he is a different person now, a different kind of Christian since he reached Bellevue la Montagne: "A little over a year ago, I changed. I still struggle to define exactly what happened, but a trip to Haiti, and The Good Neighbor Orphanage, gave me renewed purpose and passion—and to be honest, it messed me up a little. It shook me out of my comfort zone. It caused me to question my career and my purpose. It raised concerns about how I live and the excess in my life."[10]

Do you see where I'm headed with this? If we stay in the DR—whatever internal place we've gotten to—where it's safe, if we never cross the border, if we only go halfway—then Jeff experiences no life change. He—like countless others—remains glibly content with his spirituality the way it used to be.

But things change for everyone when we reach the top of the mountain called Beautiful.

Together let's explore this compelling path of spirituality that bends toward justice. For everyone who feels stuck, for all who are stagnant, for all who dream of a more vibrant life—for more meaning, a more robust spirituality, a more daring faith.

Part 1

Passion Stage:
The Quest for Purpose

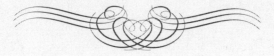

I was driving my wife to the Nashville airport with my friend Jim in the car. Just before we exited the freeway we passed a young twentysomething girl dragging a large black suitcase and an overstuffed duffel bag down the freeway shoulder.

"What was that?" I exclaimed. "I think she's walking to Nashville!" It was crazy. She had obviously walked more than a mile from the airport and was now continuing on the freeway's edge toward Music City.

After quickly dropping off Veronica, Jim and I circled back and pulled over on the shoulder next to the girl as semis blew past my rearview mirror. A guardrail separated us as Jim leaned out the window and hollered above the roaring traffic, "Are you okay?"

She looked frazzled and afraid, like a wounded sparrow

on the ground after it flies into a sliding glass door. "I'm fine," she said—but she didn't look fine.

I detected an accent, Australian I guessed. She was slender and young, and looked like she could be on her way to a recording audition . . . but why was she dragging two enormous pieces of luggage down the freeway shoulder?

Jim was riding shotgun—that's why he yelled out the window first. But all he did was frighten her. Even without the dark glasses and black shirt he was wearing, Jim is an intimidating man. Picture the guy your landlord would send to collect your overdue rent.

Sensing her apprehension, I leaned over Jim toward the open window and shouted, "I'm a pastor." Like that would fix everything. "We've stopped to help you. It's not safe for you here. Let us drive you to where you need to go."

She backed farther to the shoulder's edge. I felt like we were two guys holding suckers out the car window asking neighborhood children at play, "Do you want some candy?"

"A taxi is on the way to pick me up," she said.

"On the side of the freeway?" I was skeptical.

She tried waving us on, saying she was fine, when suddenly—sure enough—a taxi pulled up on the side of the freeway. The driver jumped out and ran toward her to pull her and her bulging luggage to safety.

I'm glad she got the ride she needed that day, but I imagined I saw in her a lost and frightened soul, searching for a future . . . maybe in music, maybe acting. For some reason the image of her with her bags on the side of the road struck me as symbolic. We're all like that at some level—alone on the road, heading somewhere or else standing still.

The soul needs purpose. I think that's why the compelling prophet Jeremiah wrote the words from God, "I will give you hope and a future."

More than practically anything else in this life, isn't that what we desire most? We long to know that this limited career or limited circle of friends or limited town is not the end.

We long for more, for a future with *purpose*.

Passion Stage

The passion stage of faith describes the period in a person's life when the longing for a God-given destiny emerges. The soul longs for a future. The soul wants more.

However, this is the very reason so many remain stuck and stagnate at stage 3 (Relational Faith). They believe the greater life, the life they've always wanted, is too elusive, too unattainable. So they give up, they settle. They atrophy.

But for those who believe the words of Jesus when He says, "Enter into my kingdom,"[1] this stage is for you.

This is the stage that crafts us, shapes our future, molds the soul. Fowler explains that through this passion stage, people "make critical choices about the defining elements of their identity and faith."[2]

This stage is about dreaming and doing.

In her seminal work on this formative life stage, *The Critical Years*, Sharon Parks writes, "A central strength of the young adult is the capacity to respond to *visions of the world as it might become* [emphasis mine]. This is the time in every generation for renewal of the human vision."[3]

Speaker and writer Louie Giglio has realized this. He saw that eighteen- to-twenty-eight-year-olds were prepared to go anywhere, do anything they felt Jesus calling them to. So Louie started a millennial movement, he calls it the Passion Movement, and it's swelling.

The passion stage is when we begin seeking our divine destiny and seize our divine moment. We all have this deep desire to discover a life of significance, a life filled with purpose and passion—now is the time when that quest must begin.

Visions of the World As It Might Be

I'm on social media—Facebook, Twitter, Instagram, you name it. And I hear the desire of the next-generation Christian on social media crying out, "Do you see me? Do you hear me? Do I matter?"

I think the last question reveals the deepest longing of our souls.

Every one of us wants to know that our one life is not a wasted life, a meaningless life.

Generations past may have been okay with punching the clock, doing the nine-to-five. Not the church of the present.

This next generation is ready to give their lives to bending the moral arc of the universe toward justice. They believe they can remake the world into something good and beautiful as God originally intended. They long for purpose and seek a church that will show them the way.

Don't we all?

This is what is so powerful about this passion stage: people in it—for the first time in their lives—begin to dream of a world as God intended. This is the stage of limitless possibilities, the stage where hopes and dreams come alive. This is the stage when childlike faith is actually lived and people begin to do the things for God they once believed were impossible or only imagined someone else could accomplish.

Chapter 3

JUSTICE CALLING

I had known Bill Clark for most of my life, even lived with his family in Liberia for a year of high school, so I was not surprised when he and his wife, Pat, decided to move back to Africa when he was seventy-five years old.

Bill had not been in Malawi long before he began calling his son, Chris, my lifelong friend, to tell him about the trouble in Malawi. Bill called at least once a week, usually weeping. Bill would say, "Chris, there are orphans everywhere. They are sleeping on the streets. No one seems to care. You need to come and help take care of them."

Bill was right. The orphan problem in Malawi had turned pandemic. AIDS was ravaging the nation. In a country of twelve million, more than a million were orphaned by AIDS. Mothers and fathers were dying by the thousands.

Finally, Chris agreed to load a forty-foot shipping container with supplies for kids—he thought that would help. Then he flew nine thousand miles to help distribute the goods. But when Chris landed in Malawi, everything changed. He *saw* that all the things his father had said were true. Hundreds of orphans wandered helpless in every village he visited, scavenging for food. Sleeping in the open air. Wearing rags. Sick. It broke his heart. And Chris began to cry like his father.

Chris had the job in Seattle every young Christian dreams, an area director for Youth for Christ; he worked with students, ran camps, led cross-country trips for hundreds to national conferences. But the calling to Africa was too strong. So he quit his day job and started a nonprofit (Children of the Nations) to care for orphans in Africa. He's kept it up for more than twenty years. He built orphanages and homes and found parents for countless children. The calling was too great, too strong to ignore.

I wonder, what are you doing with your life for God, right now, that is making you uncomfortable? What are you doing with your life for God, right now, that scares you? Because if your dreams do not frighten you, then maybe your dreams are too small.

Your justice calling will not be easy. If it were easy, everyone would be doing it. Your calling will be a bit audacious, a little ridiculous, radical, and out of the ordinary. But it will also be right, because it will be exactly where God wants you to be.

Your justice calling will put you where your greatest passion and your greatest strength intersect to meet God's kingdom plan for ending the injustice and healing His world. God made you full of purpose and gave you certain strengths. Your purpose is unique to you. God has weighed your heart with things others don't care about so much.

Has God put you here to be an advocate for the marginalized immigrant, a voice for the rights of women—because you've seen a woman's rights trampled on? Has He given you a heart for the parentless and for orphaned children—because children have not arrived easily in your own arms? Is He inspiring you to defend the underpaid worker, end the sex trade of children and young women, discover sustainable food sources for the hungry or clean water for entire communities? What makes your heart tender—or makes it burn?

Bible writers like Isaiah and James say to care about more than just your own private spirituality; true religion involves the pursuit of justice and showing compassion.[1]

You are God's plan for stopping injustice and ending oppression on earth. This means at your very core you'll be fundamentally bothered by oppression. It means confronting oppression when you see it, and giving your best effort to helping society regain its moral equilibrium.

Your justice calling is what the passion stage is all about.

The more you respond to your justice calling, the more you live by faith. Passionately.

Maybe you've felt a calling sear your soul. Maybe you have ignored it for years, hoping it would fade away, but the burning only intensifies. Or maybe you're just now starting to see the smoke. The only thing that can heal that soul burn is a life drenched in the divine pursuit of remaking this world.

If you're just now starting to see the smoke rising in the distance, but your justice calling still isn't clear, here are a few ways to get started and gain clarity:

Get Up and Get Out

God will not inspire you to act from the recliner or while sitting in an adult Sunday school class. It's time for you to get up and go . . . into the blighted neighborhood near you. Across town and across oceans. When you are moving and seeing and serving, then God can work in you.

Bill and Jeanne are successful commercial Realtors, but Bill said he felt God wanted to do more through his life. So Bill signed up to travel with our team to Liberia, and Jeanne signed up for our abolitionist work in Thailand.

Bill and Jeanne came home inspired. Together they told

me God was clearly telling them to adopt an orphan from Liberia, even though they were in their fifties. They soon realized adopting from Liberia was practically impossible. They grew increasingly frustrated and confused by what they sensed was God's clear leading.

Then two weeks ago a friend from our church approached them about taking in a sixteen-year-old parentless girl from inner-city Phoenix. At first they were hesitant. Then it hit them both, this is God speaking. This is God leading. This is our calling.

Bill and Jeanne said yes.

Think about this: a couple leaves their life of comfort and luxury in search of their justice calling in Africa and Asia, and God says their calling is in the city next door.

They hear Him, and do it.

But none of these beautiful things happen until they get up, get out, and go!

People First

We often look around at the world, wondering what cause does God have for me? It doesn't work like that. Stop standing at a distance and start giving your life to cross-racial, cross-ethnic, cross-neighborhood relationships and friendships and community gatherings.

If these stories seem too big or remote right now, don't

be discouraged. It's okay to start small. You do not have to first choose a *cause* or an *issue*—those kinds of things will choose you. The key is to first give yourself to knowing and loving people. Authentic justice begins face-to-face.

Listen to His Spirit

You want to ignore him, I know. No one wants to be *called* to the Tijuana slums or the meth hills of rural Kentucky. That's why we ignore the spirit of God.

Often, people see the oppression all around and do nothing. This has been the case for centuries. Solomon in the Bible writes, "Again I looked and saw all the oppression that was taking place under the sun: I saw the tears of the oppressed, and they have no comforter; power was on the side of their oppressors, and they have no comforter."[2]

Two thousand years ago, there was a community of people who were so influenced by the Spirit of God that racial barriers began to come down. No one had seen anything like this before. Jews having dinner with Greeks! They began using family language, like brothers and sisters, to refer to one another. People began to loosen the grip on their possessions, they shared, they lived simply. And they served each other.

No one could imagine that a group of people would treat each other with so much kindness, grace, dignity, respect . . . and love. It was like heaven.

It happened two thousand years ago, it can happen again, it's happening.

I invite you to give your life to that kind of church, that kind of Christianity, that kind of life.

Use Your Abilities

You are better at some things than everybody else. You are a pro where others are amateurs. You know more about medicine, or mechanics, drilling for water or drilling cavities, construction or corn harvesting, microeconomics or malnutrition, or solar or sanitation . . . than anybody else. You are good at it. And you know it, we know it, God knows it.

As Western Christians, we have the ability and influence to make so much change for good; all that is usually required is the will and determination.

I know this because I've seen it happen, like a few years ago in Africa.

Rushing into the Malawian college's dining hall and interrupting my breakfast, one of the faculty blurted, "Palmer, your people are nuts! They're asking me where they can find an ATM to withdraw enough cash to dig a well. That's 150,000 Malawian kwachas, around $10,000! Are they crazy?"

Yes, in the best of ways. I went to find Paul.

Paul's on my staff. I hired him from Guatemala. He was

our leader for this team of sixty-two people in Malawi. "What is this I hear about our people wanting to withdraw ten thousand dollars from an ATM . . . here in Lilongwe? We're all gonna get beat down and robbed," I joked.

Paul tried to explain that while they were in the community of Chimpampha the previous afternoon, a number of our people had approached him to ask if we could dig a well for the village, since the people were drinking water from a swamp. So that night Paul invited the sixty-two from The Grove—the Phoenix-area church I help lead—to email, Facebook, text, Pinterest, and tweet their friends (and, I guess, also find an ATM) to see if together they could come up with ten thousand dollars . . . in three days.

When Paul saw the frustrated look on my face, he interrupted. "We already have half of it!"

"In one night?" I questioned.

"Yes, in one night."

It didn't sound like a great plan, but I told him to try raising the money and getting the well dug, as long as they stayed away from the ATMs.

Through everyone's friends and social networks, the money poured in. Two days later, they had ten thousand dollars. Four days after that, before the team of sixty-two boarded the plane for America, the people of Chimpampha were pumping crystal-clear water out of a shiny new pump in the middle of their village.

Now I dare you to say, "God, here is my very best. Take it, use it."

Remember, this does not have to be something grand and audacious or in faraway places. In fact, this kind of life begins now, right where you are.

If you are mechanically inclined, invite friends to help you repair single mothers' cars when they break down.

If you know English, begin tutoring immigrants to help them transition and find work.

If you love growing things, start a community garden near your neighborhood or a sustainable urban garden in a blighted corner of town.

If you can write, start a blog. Write about what must change in your community to stop discrimination and end inequality.

If you are an artist, start to paint, make music, take pictures, write prose. Let God use your passion as His canvas for justice.

Jacob in the Bible had a dream. He was on the run, aimless and wandering, when he dreamed of the kingdom of heaven touching earth. He woke up to a fight—literally—a fight with God for his life.

God won.

And God went on to tell Jacob something we all need to

hear: *You are made for more! Your life is meant for something astonishing.*

Bethel, the place where Jacob wrestled God, became a place of transformation. God stepped down from heaven to put one man back on course. The aimless wanderer turned and rose to lead a nation.

If you're not sure, if you're feeling aimless, if you're even on the run from some problem or person or from God Himself—ask God. Ask if He has something larger, something more, something surprising, something full of purpose for you!

Chapter 4

DREAM LIFE

His name was Sixto Rodriguez. He sang like a rock star.

Rodriguez began writing music at the peak of Detroit's music era. This was the early 1970s, when Motown Records was pumping out hit after hit.

Playing nightclubs, bars, and just about any venue that would have him, Rodriguez began to grow a reputation. Word soon spread to the recording studios of Detroit about this quiet stoic from the raw streets of Detroit who wrote poetic prose and sang with a crisp, rich, mesmerizing voice—but was playing all this astonishing music for drunk dockworkers in places like a bar named the Sewer.

On a foggy January night, two young recording executives went searching for this mysterious Rodriguez. They found him in the Sewer, sitting in a chair with his back to the ambivalent audience, who filled the dark room with thick clouds of cigarette smoke . . . but the sound was riveting, the lyrics equally compelling. They signed him to a two-album contract with Sussex Records and started making music.

Sixto's dream had come true.

The release of Rodriguez's first album, *Cold Fact*, was a stone-cold failure. It received practically no radio play. Some said it was his lack of onstage charisma. Some said he didn't fit neatly into either pop-rock or R & B genres.

In 1971, Rodriguez released his second album, *Coming from Reality*. The sales were equally dismal. Promoters tried a West Coast tour, but he continued to play with his back to the audience and lacked the stage presence to energize a crowd. The tour bombed.

Two weeks before Christmas, Sussex dropped him, turning prophetic the lines of his song "Cause": "*'Cause I lost my job two weeks before Christmas.*"

No one was really sure what happened, but word on the street was that the crowd had booed Sixto as he played song after song that he had poured his soul into. That's why, so the story goes, at the end of his set, despondent and dejected, failing at what he loved most, Rodriguez pulled out a gun and shot himself in the head.

Socrates was right: the mob is always wrong.

But the story doesn't end here.

In the summer of '72, a young American high school girl traveled to South Africa and brought a copy of *Cold Fact*. When she played it for her new crowd of friends they demanded copies. Bootlegged cassettes spread like a virus across South Africa, and radio DJs were driven mad by teenagers demanding radio play of songs like "I Wonder."

By 1973, Rodriguez's music dominated the airwaves of South Africa.

As the record stores and radio stations scrambled to find distribution channels for Rodriguez's music in South Africa, the heavy-handed apartheid government banned radio play of "I Wonder." To ensure the DJs honored the prohibition, government enforcers scratched out the song on the vinyl record with a nail.

But all this did was turn teenagers rabid for uncensored bootleg copies.

In places like Durban, not only was Rodriguez's music outselling any other Detroit artist, but as the youth of South Africa began to turn against the oppressive apartheid regime, Rodriguez's music became their anthem.

Raised in poverty-stricken inner-city Detroit, Rodriguez was a voice for the poor and oppressed. His antiestablishment themes resonated with South Africa's marginalized. They sang his music as songs of rebellion like "I Wonder," with its iconic line, *"I wonder if this hatred will ever end."*

South Africans say that for more than a decade Rodriguez's music pounded the walls of every party, every gathering, every political rally, and practically every home in the nation.

In the early eighties, a young South African from Johannesburg, Steven Segerman—nicknamed Sugarman, after Sixto's hit, "Sugar Man"—moved to Cape Town and opened a music store to feature Rodriguez's music. There he connected with investigative journalist Craig Strydom to finally find out what had become of the mysterious Rodriguez. In 1997 they put up a website to help in the search for the truth about Sixto. After just a few months, Sugarman received a short email:

> "Sixto is alive and well; he's my father. But some things are better left a mystery."

Sugarman had grown tired of the mystery and wanted the truth about the man and his music that had shaped a generation and a country. After a flurry of emails, Rodriguez's daughter arranged a phone call. Sugarman could hardly believe what he was hearing as Rodriguez greeted him over the phone. Sugarman fired a barrage of questions.

"Where have you been? Why did you stop making music? Will you come to South Africa and play for the millions of admirers who will celebrate that you are alive?"

When Rodriguez finally hung up the phone, he turned to his daughter and said, with wonder lingering in his voice, "He is telling me that in South Africa—I'm bigger than Elvis."

When his album fizzled and the crowds booed, Rodriguez quit making music—no, there was never a gun onstage. That part of the legend wasn't true. But Rodriguez needed to feed his young family, so he put down the guitar and picked up a sledgehammer and began demoing houses in Detroit's crumbling inner city.

For decades. Never hearing. Never knowing. That in Cape Town he was a rock star bigger than the King.

After the midnight phone call, Sugarman flew from Cape Town to Detroit to meet the mysterious rock star.

When Sugarman found him he was living alone in abject poverty.

He had not written a note or lyric in twenty-five years. Most days his guitar sat idle in the corner collecting dust. He was gaunt and tired; the years of swinging a sledgehammer were taking their toll.

"Come to Cape Town," Sugarman urged. "Three generations have been raised on your music. We will fill the concert hall with people who cannot wait to know that you are alive and to hear you sing." He finally said yes.

When Sixto walked onstage at the concert hall in South Africa, the five-thousand-seat-capacity crowd erupted. The bass player played the first eight notes of "I Wonder," but the crowd was too loud for Rodriguez to begin singing. They waved and cheered, and many cried as they welcomed Rodriguez, who for two decades a nation believed was dead.

For more than fifteen minutes the crowed refused to be

silenced, and Rodriguez stood speechless—taking it all in, trying to believe that his dream really had come true.

Everybody Dreams

Maybe Rodriguez's story is your story.

Perhaps you've been demoing abandoned houses in Detroit when you could have been making music by the beach in Cape Town.

Maybe it's time to stop listening to the critics who say, "Put down the guitar and pick up a sledgehammer."

It's time to move from the limited life to the life of limitless possibilities.

We often live with too low a view of our own lives. We think we can't make a difference. We believe the problems of this world are too big for one person to tackle. It's time to change our thinking. You are the one prized by God. You are the apple of His eye. You—not the billions, but you—are the reason His son stepped down from heaven. So give this world all you've got. Stop holding back. Stop waiting for someone else.

We all have two lives we can live. There's the life you live every day. The life that many times ends up becoming a tired rut, sapping you of every ounce of creative passion. But then there's the life you dream of living. That's the second life. For many, it's the life unlived.

Josh was living that unlived life, as a barista in a coffee shop. There's nothing wrong with making coffee, but there's a difference between a period of waiting and a lifetime of it. Josh had music on the inside, and he didn't need to wait any longer. Finally, he quit making coffee and started writing music. He took another barista, Matt, with him and started a band—The Afters.

Now he makes music for a living and their songs are national hits. He tours the country and the world sharing his music, changing lives. It's good and beautiful.

I met Josh on a tour. Now we work together at church, and every week we all get to hear Josh's music.

Maybe that's you. Maybe there is something beautiful on the inside that needs to come out.

I think all of us end up demoing houses in Detroit when we stop believing, when we stop dreaming, when we stop making music.

If that is you today, then it's time to get out of Detroit.

Because there's a version of you that shines when you create, compose, and sing your songs. Every once in a while the best version of you shines through. We get glimpses of the very best you.

The *you* you dreamed of being. The you God made you to be.

We have a dirty town two hours west of Phoenix called Quartzsite. If I stop for gas there I always wonder, who lives here? Where do they come from? Why? What could possibly drive them to this kind of desolate place? It's nothing but rocks, dirt, and cacti.

But people are there. Living. Existing.

During the winters, Quartzsite fills with thousands of motor homes and RVs with people trying to escape the cold in places like Waukegan and Kalamazoo.

I'm told the American dream is to retire, buy an RV, and spend winters in towns like Quartzsite.

Sounds to me like more of a nightmare.

The ancient leader Moses was raised in a palace of potential. With Pharaoh as his adoptive father, opportunities were limitless. But Moses lost it, like so many of us do. He lost his temper and lost his reputation, lost his future. Lost it all. So he put in forty years in Quartzsite . . . until God showed up, smack-dab in front of him, and said, "Lead!"

Get out of the desert—get out of Detroit or Quartzsite

or wherever you are simply putting in time—and lead God's people toward something better, something new, something spectacular.

<hr>

Some dreams actually come true, like Martin Luther King, Jr.'s.

Fifty years ago, from the steps of the Lincoln Memorial, overlooking the Washington, DC, mall, MLK shared his dream—the dream of a lifetime.

"I have a dream," he announced, "that my four little children will one day live in a nation where they will not be judged by the color of their skin but by the content of their character."

We don't have it perfect yet, but I see his dream coming true.

I say that because most of the athletes, celebrities, and leaders our children—my children—admire and want to emulate are African American. Their favorite people require only the mention of a first name, or a couple of letters: They want to hit a golf ball like Tiger. Shoot like LeBron. Sing like Beyoncé or Usher. Inspire like Oprah. Deliver a line like Denzel. Do you see how this world, this country, this church is different because of one man living God's dream life?

Cultural architect Erwin McManus says:

A dreamer [is one] who dreams.

A dreamer [is one] who dreams of a better world.

A dreamer [is one] who dreams of a better world and
risks everything to make it happen.[1]

That is Martin Luther King, Jr.'s story.

When you begin to live God's dream life, there is no more drifting, no more wandering, no more emptiness. Instead, you know with confidence, *this is why I was made; this is the reason for my life*.

Dreams give us energy, direction, inspiration, and a reason to get out of bed in the morning.

The Bible says that without a dream the people perish. When you stop dreaming, your work turns into a rut.

When you stop dreaming, your marriage has half a chance of making it.

When you stop dreaming, people frustrate you and relationships turn septic.

When you stop dreaming, your children drop out of school, because you paint them no future.

When you stop dreaming, you watch the clock, get by, pay the bills . . . and your soul shrivels and future fades.

Dreams are not reserved for iconic leaders like Martin Luther King, Jr.—you can dream, too.

All people created by God have this deep longing for an extraordinary life full of purpose. All of us dream great dreams.

Some are broken . . . *but everybody dreams*. Some are

lost . . . *but everybody dreams.* Some are forgotten . . . *but everybody dreams.*

Some are fading away . . . *but everybody dreams.*

The brilliant theologian Scot McKnight writes:[2]

> At the core of every dream you have,
> Behind every dream you have, Ahead of every dream
> others have,
> And in the center of every good dream every human
> has . . .
> We will find the kingdom dream of Jesus.

We are designed to give our one life to that dream.

When you find it, give your entire life to the dream God has embedded in your soul. And when you do, everything else begins to fall in place.

If you are wondering where to begin, start here: what is so valuable, what is so great, so important that you would give your one life to it?

God uses our dreams best when they are for His kingdom. Behind everything good and beautiful in this world is God's dream of His kingdom on earth.

The great characters in all stories are the ones who give their lives to something larger than themselves.

We see this truth repeated, time and again, in the Bible. Jacob dreamed about heaven coming to earth.

Joseph (OT Joe) explained and fulfilled dreams of feeding hungry people.

Nehemiah dreamed of rebuilding crumbled cities, like Jerusalem . . . or Port-au-Prince.

Joseph (NT Joe) dreamed of a savior who would turn the world from the worst to the best.

Peter dreamed of a new society where people of every race and ethnicity would sit around tables as one.

Paul dreamed of crossing seas to carry good news to people on distant shores.

John dreamed of a new earth where the tears of the poor and the broken are wiped away.

Some dreams are so powerful you can't leave them in your sleep.

God has made you a creative person with a unique set of gifts. You do some things better than everyone else. You have a passion God has embedded in your soul. Maybe you are an artist or a writer; maybe you can build things or stand up and give speeches. Maybe you are a photographer or a painter. It could be you have a natural gift for leading; people follow you. You're a kid magnet whom high schoolers rally around. Maybe you know more about fast-pitch softball than most college coaches. Maybe, since you were eight, you've dreamed of flying, hiking the Himalayas, teaching English in China, or leading white-water rafting trips down the Zambezi.

The problem is, somewhere along the way you gave up on your dream. Someone criticized you. Someone did not believe in you. Someone rejected your application. Someone told you that you were not smart enough, or that you could not afford it. Somebody cut you during tryouts. Somebody gave you a D. Someone gave the job to somebody else.

And you listened. You believed the critics and the skeptics. So you quit. You gave up. You stopped the dreaming and believing. You stopped making music. You settled for a life less wonderful.

We do that, don't we? We let the car payment, the job security, the kids' needs, life itself—keep us from the dreams we know God destined us for.

"Livin' the dream!"

That's how the trainer at my gym said it.

All I had asked was, "How are you doing, man?" I loved his answer.

I wondered if I was.

I wonder if you are.

I wonder how different life would be had you pursued the

dream life God planned for you. I wonder who you would be, what you would become, if you believed. Believed that he has a hope and a future for you that is fulfilling and flourishing.

In his song "I Wonder," Rodriguez sings, "*I wonder how many dreams have gone bad.*"

I wonder how many dreams of yours have gone bad.

I wonder if we are even slightly convinced that God has the very best future waiting for us. I wonder if we actually believe the promises of the Bible that God can do great things through our lives.

Like when He says in the book of Isaiah, "So you'll go out in joy, you'll be led into a whole and complete life. The mountains and hills will lead the parade, bursting with song. All the trees of the forest will join the procession, exuberant with applause." God is making clear that He has this good and beautiful plan for your life.

Know that God has that livin'-the-dream life waiting for you.

Jesus came to liberate and inspire people to a new kind of life, the kind in which you fully live. Writers of the Bible, like Jeremiah, keep reminding us of this, "I have it all planned out—plans to take care of you, not abandon you, plans to give you the future you hope for."[3]

It's never too late, the ancient prophet Joel says: "And afterward, I will pour out my Spirit on all people. Your sons and daughters will prophesy, your old men will dream dreams, your young men will see visions."[4]

So dream new dreams. See what everyone else can't. Believe the impossible will happen.

❧

My brother-in-law, Steve Spencer, was in Uganda, helping to build a third African Bible College campus, when Bob Goff, best-selling author and founder of Restore International, came to visit. They met with a distinguished member of parliament who was under tremendous pressure because of his Christian faith. It even looked like he would soon lose his job.

Sitting in a small restaurant over drinks, Steve says the man seemed defeated, tired, beat down, and worn-out, when Bob asked him, "So it looks like you may not be in politics much longer. What do you dream about doing next?"

The politician answered with something very general, like doing more to help the youth in Uganda.

"No, no!" Bob interrupted. "What are your dreams?" Leaning over the table, Bob asked again, "What fills your imagination when you lie in bed at night? Your dreams, your dreams!"

A giant smile grew over the Ugandan's face; he sat up straight and excitedly blurted, "I've always wanted to play the guitar in a band!"

"That's what I'm talking about!" Bob exclaimed. "That's it! Do you know how to play the guitar?"

"No," he replied.

"Do you own a guitar?"

"No."

"Well, I'll pay for lessons," Bob promised. "And as soon as I land in the U.S., I'm mailing you a guitar! What kind of music do you like? What do you want to play on your guitar?"

"Well," the politician said, "I don't have very many CDs, but the one I listen to most is by a Christian musician— I don't know if you have heard of him—Brandon Heath. He's my favorite. I would love to learn to play Brandon Heath's music."

"Brandon! Hang on."

Bob whipped out his cell phone and dialed . . . "Brandon . . . yeah, I know I woke you up. I'm in Uganda. Hey, I need you to talk to a friend of mine here who wants to learn to play the guitar. Would you say hi and tell him he can do it!?" The politician's eyes were the size of saucers, Steve says, and his smile even bigger, as Brandon Heath encouraged him to live his dream (when I was with Brandon last month, I asked him to retell the story. So awesome!).

Maybe you don't know Brandon or Bob. That's okay. But we all know somebody who can help us inspire someone. We can all learn from Bob: he never takes no for an answer, he never believes anything is impossible, and he always sees the best in everyone.

So can you.

Turn Your Nightmares into Dreams

Christmas is a time for dreaming. That's why we read poems at Christmastime with lines like: "The children were nestled all snug in their beds, while visions of sugarplums danced in their heads."

When we retell the original Christmas story from the Bible, we usually tell it bright and cheery. We breeze past lines like "His fiancée is pregnant . . . and he knows the baby is not his!"[5] That's not a dream; that sounds more like a nightmare.

We don't think much, either, of the words we read in Luke: "Mary was greatly troubled . . ."[6] Of course she was! This was not the life of Mary's dreams. Let's put the story in the context of a sixteen-year-old girl in first-century Middle East. Mary lived in the land of the Talmud, a world of exacting standards and regulations.

The Bible says Mary was engaged. "Engaged" in ancient Hebrew culture, however, is not the same as "engaged" today. For a Jew, being engaged was the equivalent of being married . . . except couples could not share a bed.

If Mary was pregnant, then she was an adulteress. The Torah called for her to be stoned. If adultery could not be proven, then she would be given the bitter-water test. Numbers instructs if she becomes sick, then she is guilty. If she does not, she is innocent.

In Mary's day, the bitter-water test had become a way to

humiliate young women, a way to intimidate others into being faithful to their engagements or husbands. The priest would drag the accused woman to the city gate. Then, with her hair let down, clothes ripped, and jewelry torn off, bystanders were encouraged to mock and spit.

She would remain there the entire day, a warning to all "loose" women. People would call her *sotah*, meaning "suspected adulteress," even if the charge was unfounded.

Sotah was a curse not only for Mary but for Joseph as well. His reputation would be ruined. His friends would question his manhood. Her son—Jesus—would be known as *mamzer*, the illegitimate one.

Gabriel says, "This is news of great joy." Really?

Maybe your dream life has turned into a nightmare. A son rebelled. Your job turned bitter. Someone talked you into the wrong dream. Or someone talked you out of your dream—it was too big, they said. And you believed them.

In the musical *Les Misérables*, the song "I Dreamed a Dream" contains the lyrics, "*I had a dream my life would be so different from this hell I'm living. . . . Now life has killed the dream.*"[7]

But it doesn't have to end this way. You don't have to resign yourself to the nightmare of your circumstances. Every person who has ever done anything significant for God has had to take risks and find courage to overcome. That's why the angel said to Joseph, "Do not be afraid."

The entire Bible is a story of courage and faith. The

writer of Hebrews made this list of the most courageous. About Abraham he writes, "When he left he had no idea where he was going." Who does that? The person living God's dream life.

Courage is a dream-life essential. God's kind of dream life takes guts and faith.

Joseph ignored friends' warnings when they most likely encouraged him to walk out on Mary. Instead, he walked toward Bethlehem. He made the long, dark walk of faith. Toward the life he knew God had planned for him . . . and his son.

No matter what has happened to your dreams of the past, remember this: somewhere in the middle of all the dreams you dream is the life God has waiting for you.

Discover it, embrace it.

Don't stop dreaming

Don't let the music die on the inside.

If you want to step into this next faith stage, it begins with pursuing your dream. Actually doing what God has burned in your soul. This is the moment. Now is the time. Today is the day.

Register your nonprofit. Build the website.

Quit your day job. Get on the plane. Make the call.

Put up your money, every last cent.

And live the dream life that only God in heaven Himself could have seared on your soul.

It's time to dream. Don't quit halfway; pursue your dreams and passions all the way to your divine destiny—carry on.

Chapter 5

WRITE A MILLION WORDS

I was having lunch with author Ted Dekker recently and asked him the question I love asking creatives: How did you become a writer?

Ted is an expatriate. He was born in the remote New Guinea village of Kanggime.

His answer was intriguing. Ted said he wasn't always a writer. A business major in college, Ted jumped straight into marketing. Immediately he knew he was good at it. Maybe it was a skill he learned from the Irian Jaya traders in the Baliem Valley.

By age thirty, however, Ted felt increasingly drawn to his greatest passion—writing. He had never studied to be a writer, was never employed as a writer, or even had an article published. But he felt God had filled his soul with a story that had to be told.

So he quit the marketing business, and he and his wife pooled all they had to pay cash for a small home outside of Austin, where Ted started to write.

His first novel, *Heaven's Wager*, was rejected by every publisher that read it. So Ted wrote a second novel. No better luck. Rejection again. Ted wrote a third and a fourth. In fact, Ted said he wrote more than a million words—literally—before a publisher bit.

And then he sold a million books.

Ten Thousand Hours

Lives of remarkable purpose demand hard work.

No one falls backward into—or stumbles upon—a life of great purpose. Great purpose is always preceded by determined, impassioned, relentless effort.

Never underestimate the value of hard work.

There is no substitute for the sheer determination to outwork everybody else out there. Behind every great career, brilliant scientist, gifted musician, number one draft pick, first chair, Broadway actor, first place, Hall of Famer, is countless hours of relentless hard work.

Nobody wakes up one morning with enough raw talent

to make the PGA Tour or fill a concert hall. You must first put in the time.

Do it. Every day. For years. Not just casually, but with intention, and with expert coaching to improve.

We are often under the impression that brilliantly talented people are born with their abilities. That is rarely—practically never—the truth.

Malcolm Gladwell says it takes ten thousand hours to reach the top of your field. Whether it's starting in Little League baseball to reach the majors, spending time on the violin to one day play with the New York Philharmonic, or putting in hours in the kitchen to wear the prestigious red, white, and blue collar of the Meilleurs Ouvriers de France.

Winston Churchill said he never gave an impromptu answer, interview, or speech. He would often seem as though he was fumbling for words or needed to pause, but that was just an act. Every "impromptu" speech he ever gave, he first rehearsed a hundred times in front of the mirror.

He would even practice answers to the questions he knew reporters would ask when he walked out the front door of Downing Street first thing in the morning.

Billy Graham says he preached more sermons to the loblolly pines on the hillside behind his home in Charlotte than to people.

Forty years ago, Herbert Simon and William Chase published a paper in *American Scientist*, sharing the famous findings of their study on the game of chess:

There are no instant experts in chess—certainly no instant masters or grandmasters. There appears not to be on record any case (including Bobby Fischer) where a person reached grandmaster level with less than about a decade's intense preoccupation with the game. We would estimate, very roughly, that a master has spent perhaps 10,000 to 50,000 hours staring at chess positions.[1]

I heard a famous radio talk show host once respond to a caller who tried to use humor on air, much in the same way the talk show host did every day. After a long—uncomfortably long—pause, the host dryly said (I'm paraphrasing from memory), "I know I make my job sound easy. To the average listener, it seems like anyone could do what I do. But it has taken me years and years of practice to be both snide and funny, intelligent and snarky, insightful and witty. So let's leave the entertainment portion of the program to me. Just ask the question."

Cruel, funny, and true.

And it's not simply putting in the ten thousand hours that puts a person at the top of their field. As Malcolm Gladwell says, "It's talent plus preparation."[2]

For example, you can run for ten thousand hours, but that won't make you an Olympic sprinter.

Somewhere on the inside you are born with a gift, a talent, an ability that sets you apart. Something that, when you combine it with hard work, you thrive and flourish and excel in.

You might be a gifted writer, or have an eye for fashion, or naturally can find the perfect pitch, or have a knack for organization, or are a born leader . . . now go out and do it. Write a million words. Practice for ten thousand hours.

Resolve

Whatever you do, don't bury it.

That was Jesus' warning about wasting purpose and potential.

In the book of Matthew, Jesus spoke of three men challenged with a task. Two gave their best efforts and hearts. One, however, did nothing. He buried his talent—literally. He sat on his hands. Refused to do the heavy lifting. He did nothing, yet still expected praise. He was a bum.

Some people take their talent and grow it, develop it. They thrive. Some people, on the other hand, take their talent and bury it. They never do much at all to make it grow and flourish. Jesus says those kinds of people live far from the kingdom of God.

The kingdom of God is a kingdom of thriving.

So when the one man does nothing to propel the kingdom forward, Jesus says, "Kick the bum out."

We must be careful not to become the same. Rather

than investing in the purposes God has given us or putting in the ten thousand hours, too many of us follow the way of the bum in Jesus' story and bury our dreams, our potential. We simply quit and give up.

So many fall short of the upper stages of faith, because we stop believing God has something dramatic, daring, even dangerous that He wants us to do in this world for Him.

Here's the question for all of us: Is there only one record label?

I understand that life gets practical. You've gotta pay the rent. Or you fall in love and want to get married, but you don't have a "real job." The responsible thing is to find an income—any income sometimes will do. So we quit. We settle. We abandon our dreams, our passions, our gifts from God to make the monthly payment on a minivan we hated the day we drove it off the lot.

I'm not sure which dreams feel unlived for you. They could be dreams from long ago when you were young, they could be brand-new frightening ones God is just starting to show you.

Either way, don't give up so easily on God's dream life. Find resolve.

This faith stage is about living full of purpose and passion for God, and finding resolve. It's about hearing the call of God and then actually pursuing it. This is the *all-in* stage. The stage when you live so confident of the hand of

God on your life you are ready to *do, go, be* whatever the call.

Giving up is easy.

Quitting demands no willpower or determination or tenacity.

Doing the things you know God put you on earth to accomplish is the hard part.

My favorite story of passionate resolve is the one about Chris Bonga and making it to communist Cuba.

I could not believe what the FedEx rep on the phone was saying.

It was ten thirty in the morning. I was standing in front of Wheaton Bible Church (near Chicago) with twenty-one college students, ready to drive to Toronto, where we would catch a plane to Havana. We were scheduled to play basketball against the Cuban Olympic team during the days and spend the evenings sharing in Cuban churches.

"Your package mistakenly went to Seattle," the agent explained.

The FedEx delivery truck was supposed to have been at the church by ten with our visas for Cuba. We had an eight-hour drive to Toronto ahead of us followed by catching our flight to Cuba.

"Well, what's the earliest you can get them to Chicago?" I pressed.

"You can pick them up at our distribution center at 9 a.m. tomorrow."

Okay, I thought, *I think I can make that work.*

I turned to one of my college ministry leaders, Chris Bonga, and said, "Instead of driving to Toronto with us right now, can I put you on a plane tomorrow at eleven?" Of course he loved the idea.

So my plan was: Chris would meet the delivery truck at the FedEx distribution center at nine, drive the forty-five minutes to O'Hare, board an eleven o'clock flight to Toronto, land at noon, and hand us our visas before our plane took off at one o'clock! It was a great plan . . . kind of.

With as much confidence as I could fake, I turned to the enthusiastic college students and said, "Load up. Chris will meet us at the Toronto airport tomorrow with our visas."

And we left.

It was a bad plan, the worst of plans. What if I drove twenty people eight hours, and we didn't end up making the flight? How humiliating. How dumb. The sensible thing would be to postpone the trip. Reschedule. But quitting is easy. In college ministry, I always said, "Stick with the plan." So we did.

At midnight, bleary-eyed and cranky from the numbing drive, everyone flopped down in a musty Toronto guesthouse. Emotionally drained, I lay on the rock-hard tile floor, trying to fall asleep. I couldn't. All I could think about was the humbling drive of shame back to Chicago when our visas failed to arrive.

The next morning, I woke everyone up early and read to the students from Joshua, the part about God taking his people across the Jordan into the land of impossibility. I told them that's what flying to Cuba would be like . . . I tried to sound hopeful and full of faith—I wasn't.

At nine fifteen Chris called. I waited breathlessly for him to say he had the visas in his hand. "Palmer, I'm at the FedEx depot, but there's a problem."

"Huh? You've got to be kidding! What kind of problem?"

"The FedEx truck carrying all their parcels from the airport to the distribution center has broken down on I-355. But they're sending another truck."

"Okay," I mumbled, defeated. "If you don't have the package by nine forty-five . . . just leave, or you'll miss your flight. We'll try to get on the plane without visas."

That was another awesome idea.

Chris waited. And waited. Nine forty-five came and no package. He and his dad gave it five more minutes. At 9:50, a FedEx man walked out and handed them the visas. They jumped into the car and sped toward O'Hare.

Chris called from the car. "Okay, Palmer, I have the package with the visas."

"Did you open it just to make sure they're all there?"

"No," he said.

"Dude, count them while I'm on the phone. There should be twenty-two."

A few seconds later he almost whispered, "There are only seventeen."

"What? Count again," I said.

He was right the first time. For some reason, they'd shorted us five visas.

So I hung up and quickly dialed my contact at the Cuban Interest Section, in DC. "Rafael, there are only seventeen visas!"

"Oh yeah." He answered casually. "Havana shorted me five, and I forgot to tell you. But, Palmer, the good news is I have them right here on my desk now."

He was in DC!

"Rafael, our plane leaves in two hours. What can we do now?"

"It's not a problem, Palmer, I can just fax them to you."

Are you kidding me? Why didn't he tell me that when the first batch went to Seattle?

I gave Rafael a fax number and left our Canadian host behind to wait for the fax while we checked in at the airport.

At noon, Chris landed.

At twelve thirty, just when boarding began, our Canadian host came running up with a handful of paper. "Here's three of your visas," he stammered apologetically, handing me a wad of pages, each with a red line running down the middle. "My fax ran out of paper before all five could print."

I wanted to scream.

Instead, I turned to the two ball players who still had no visas and said, "Follow me."

We walked up to the gate agent who was checking for visas, and I waved my hand Jedi-like and said, "Their visas are waiting for them at the Havana airport. They don't need visas today."

She nodded hypnotically, and we walked past. I'm not kidding.

I had no idea what I was saying . . . but I was right. When we arrived in Havana, a military-clad officer was standing at the off-ramp with an official stamped copy of all five visas that had been sitting on Rafael's desk.

The next seven days playing basketball against the Cuban Olympic team in five different cities was one of the most exhilarating, memorable, life-altering weeks of my life. When everything seemed to be going wrong, we could have played it safe and stayed in Chicago. We could have given in to the overwhelming odds against us rather than exhausting every possibility. But we would have missed it all.

I loved sitting with Ted Dekker and hearing him say he quit his day job to pursue the purpose he knew God had for him. Who does that?

But Ted was all in; he doubled down. It was all or nothing. How much he and all his readers would have missed if he hadn't been in 110 percent!

So quit dabbling with your dreams: the part-time efforts, the halfhearted attempts. You have settled for bivocational long enough, and your dreams are turning moldy. You've been slacklining with one foot on the ground. Don't just think about what your future might be. Take action. Take risks. Live with passion. Pursue your dream, and don't quit halfway.

Chapter 6

MAKE WAVES

I want to tell you about a man with impassioned faith. A California pear grower called Jack.

Jack didn't need to farm. He had been an officer in the navy and had a business degree from San Jose State University and could have chosen to sit behind a desk in an air-conditioned office, because his grandfather owned the largest manufacturing company in the Bay Area. But Jack loved growing things and enjoyed the satisfaction of a hard day's work.

Jack says he grew up in affluence. He spent most of his time in his grandfather's backyard, playing tennis or in his country club–size swimming pool.

His family attended church occasionally, but by the time

Jack was married, he was done with that. He was busy making money, lots of it. Busy with being the president of his Rotary, and busy with annual trips to Honolulu.

When Jack turned thirty-three, that all changed. His wife, Nell, began attending a Bible study. The teaching grabbed her heart and changed her. She started to pray for Jack and bought him his first Bible. Soon God had a grip on Jack's heart, too. Three years later he gave up his lucrative pear-growing business and headed to seminary.

When Jack and Nell left their ranch home in San Jose—the one that was featured in the *South Bay Home & Garden* magazine—to go to seminary, their family thought they had gone mad. Jack's uncle was then the president of his grandfather's company, his brother owned a bank, and his father owned hundreds of acres of pear orchards in the real-estate gold mine of Silicon Valley. No one could make any sense of Jack leaving San Jose.

Jack said he was tired of the poker parties, the glad-handing at Rotary, and all the waste—all the opulence.

After seminary he began to pastor a church. But in the rural Mississippi town where he ended up, there were plenty of pastors and plenty of churches. In fact, from the front doors of Jack's Presbyterian church, you could literally throw a rock and hit the Baptist church.

Jack says he felt God could use his life for more. He felt his life was still too pedestrian, a bit too ordinary. So he left

Mississippi and moved his family across the Atlantic Ocean to Africa.

Their new home was buried deep in the West African jungle where Americans had never lived. Each Sunday he walked for miles or rode dugout canoes to preach in distant villages.

Nell—the southern belle—opened a clinic to treat malnourished babies, their mothers with malaria, and the men cut by machetes or bitten by the green mamba. Word spread quickly in the jungle. People walked for days to find a cure for everything the witch doctors could never treat. They found healing, and they found hope. The missionaries were bad for the witch-doctor business.

But the longer Jack was in the jungle, the more he realized he couldn't do it alone. He was a foreigner from America, and he felt if he could equip Africans to join in sharing this kingdom kind of life, it would spread more quickly and go further.

So Jack began to draw plans for a college, an African college to grow Christian leaders. He would bring his drawings home at night to show his family over dinner and excitedly talk of his dreams for this college.

Jack the pear grower made an appointment with the president of the country. He showed the president his plans. The president loved it.

Next, he needed half a million dollars to build the twenty-two buildings he had drawn for the new college campus. He returned to America, and in six months he founded twenty-two churches that would each pay the cost of one building. In six months, he had half a million dollars.

Jack flew back to Africa and began to build buildings. He says the only thing he had ever built before was a stable for his daughter's horse, Sir Isaac.

When Jack completed all twenty-two buildings and opened the doors of his new African college, it flourished. Students came from thousands of miles away.

But soon Jack felt one college in West Africa was not enough for a continent three times the size of America, so he built a second college in southern Africa. Then a third in East Africa. He built more than a hundred buildings on three college campuses in three different African nations.

On his college campuses, he added hospitals, radio stations, and television studios. He sent his students out each week to the prisons and orphanages and villages to love as Christ loved.

Soon thousands of his graduates were moving into positions of influence in their countries' governments, businesses, media, education, and churches.

People who hear Jack's story may question its veracity. "One pear grower from California—tired of the opulence and excess and the ordinary life—did all that?"

Yes, I know he did. I was there. Jack is my father.

Butterfly Effect

What if everything you ever did had exponential and eternal repercussions? That's the question Andy Andrews poses in his intriguing short read *The Butterfly Effect*.

He tells the captivating story of Edward Lorenz, an American mathematician and pioneer in chaos theory. Lorenz raised the preposterous idea that when a butterfly flaps its wings, it puts molecules of air in motion that, in turn, could put more molecules of air in motion. And those molecules create more movement of air, and then more, until across oceans, on the other side of the planet, a hurricane is sent spinning.

Lorenz presented his theory to a gathering of scientists, and they mocked the notion.

For twenty years his theory was left to urban legend. But then, in the mid-eighties, university physicists began to reexamine the concept. And the more they learned about cause and effect and motion, the more they realized Lorenz was right!

It's not just possible. It's not just a theory. It actually happens.

What if the life you live is like that?

What if everything you do has eternal consequences? What if every conversation matters? Not just in your life but in your children's lives, and your grandchildren's.

Would you believe me if I told you your every action has

extraordinary consequences? Most of us don't live that way. But that is how Jesus explained your life, like a planted seed.

Planting the small mustard seed is a rather pedestrian task, but then something astonishing happens. It grows ridiculously huge. Larger than any plant near it, Jesus says. It's only supposed to be a bush; now it's large enough for birds to nest in. This is unheard-of, impossible, unlikely . . . this is your life.

We think we have throwaway conversations. Throwaway moments, days . . . even years. We don't. Every day matters; every moment matters. What you do today matters forever.

C. S. Lewis liked to say, "You have never talked to a mere mortal."

So I want to remind you that you live no ordinary life. Nothing about you is insignificant. Your most simple action has exponential potential: coffee with a coworker who is down, a phone call to your son at college, inviting your next-door neighbor over for a barbecue, telling your daughter she is beautiful. Your words, your actions take root in a person's soul and grow.

I think because we believe some moments don't matter, we end up wasting careers, or we take for granted the moments with our spouse, or waste the time we have with our children.

But what if every day mattered? Every hour mattered . . . every moment mattered?

It does.

This very moment matters!

That's why I keep saying, God wants to use your life to shape and change this world.

What you do today has this ripple effect that will make waves on the other side of the world—even generations from now will be affected.

You—yes, you—can change the course of history. Your life is meant to grow and reproduce—not just pears—and multiply and influence.

Not you alone, but with God in you, you can.

Expect Incredible

Don't accept the average life. Open your eyes to a kind of spirituality that remains hidden until you begin to live a certain way. Fully live.

Kind of like Jack.

This fourth stage of faith is about living full of faith, a life of God-given purpose and limitless potential.

Too many Christians settle for an anemic life with God. Some are okay with a wasted life. Some people give up completely on the idea that they can accomplish anything meaningful or significant for God. Instead of dreaming, we turn comfortable and expect less. Don't do that.

If you take away just one truth, know that God has so

much more waiting for you. So much more that He wants to do in and through your life. I want to invite you to dream with your eyes wide open. That's how the New Testament writers talked about faith: "Now faith is being sure of what we hope for and certain of what we do not see."

People often express their craving for a deeper faith, a more mature relationship with God. So pastors do everything possible to lead people toward spiritual maturity. We offer classes, we form discipleship teams, we launch small groups, we teach, we preach, we try all the right things—and, with our fingers crossed, hope people grow.

The problem is, some think this kind of life happens inside a building where we meet once a week to sing songs, hear inspiring messages, and meet nice people. But if that is all you are doing with your faith, you have only scratched the surface.

There's a life waiting for you and me that Jesus kept talking about. He said you can make this world a bit more like heaven. He says, "Blessed are the meek, the merciful, the peacemakers."[1] When you live this way, love triumphs, grace rules, people of every race and nationality are treated with dignity, everyone shares so that no one is left without, marriages heal, families stay together.

That's God's dream for this world, and that's His dream for your life.

Chapter 7

BURN THE BOATS

In 1519, Hernán Cortés landed on the eastern sea edge of the Mayan empire—the white-sand beaches of today's Cancún—with an eleven-ship armada carrying soldiers. The Spanish had traveled Mexico a year earlier, and they were anxious to occupy it. Earlier conquistadors had been beaten back badly when they tried to take this new world, but Cortés was convinced he could win where his predecessors had lost. Cortés knew the Mayans were determined fighters and the battle ahead would be brutal. He also knew his men, like the armies before, would be tempted to lose heart and retreat to the safety of their boats, knowing the comfort of home in Europe was just a boat ride away. So he gave the order that would take away all but two options: victory or death.

He ordered his men, "Burn the boats!"

The very ships that brought them to the faraway foreign shores were burned, eliminating any notion of retreat. Removing the possibility of anything other than victory. The command could have backfired. And it almost did. Cortés and his men were later on the verge of defeat; he had no exit strategy to save their lives. They could have given up and been massacred. Incredibly, the command to burn the boats had the opposite effect on his men. Because without the boats, it was kill or be killed.

I do not share Cortés's story to glorify imperialism, but I do like his relentless determination. Too many of us too often give up too easily. We have not yet found our way to that passion stage of faith.

The Bible also carries true stories of burning all other options. In the book of Kings, we read of the ancient prophet Elijah recruiting a young apprentice named Elisha. When Elijah told Elisha of all the ways God wanted to use his life, the young man agreed to leave his family and follow Elijah. Before leaving, however, Elisha asked to return to say good-bye to his family. Elijah told him, "Go on back, but do not forget about what I have done to you." When Elisha went home, he took the plow he used to earn a living and lit it on fire. Then he killed the oxen that pulled it and threw them on the raging fire, as a sacrifice to God.

He burned plan B. He had nothing to fall back on. It was go and change a nation, or die trying.

Joshua, the commander of the Lord's army, led his followers into a similar predicament on their march to take the Promised Land. When God stopped the flow of the raging Jordan River that separated the Jews wandering in the Sinai desert from their promised land, Joshua led the masses across a dry riverbed, only to have it immediately return to flowing wildly behind them. In Joshua 3 we read, "The priests came up out of the river carrying the ark of the covenant of the Lord. No sooner had they set their feet on the dry ground than the waters of the Jordan returned to their place and ran at flood stage as before."

The water rushed in behind them . . .

There was no turning back. There was no plan B. They had crossed the Rubicon. They had passed the point of no return. They had stepped over the line in the desert sand.

Do you see where that leads us?

To a life where turning back is no longer an option.

I love it. I love it because we tend to quit too easily. I love it because we hold on to the past too long and resist embracing the future God has waiting.

How did Cortés get agreement from his men? He took away the option of failure! I read that he told his men, "If we are going home, we are going home in *their* ships." Simply awesome.

Why did they win? They had no choice! No fallback position.

We live in a culture infatuated with choices, contingency plans, and cancellation insurance. We want an option to hit *reset*, *undo*, and *rewind*. We want exit strategies and plan Bs. We have insurance that covers practically every possible catastrophe life can throw our way. Allstate calls it "mayhem," and they promise to keep it from knocking at your door . . . or crashing through your roof. Businesses have contingency plans. Factories have redundancy procedures. Equity funds and banks have risk-management departments. Investors hedge. We are a risk-averse culture.

But for some things in life, the only way out is to press further in. When we don't burn the boats and we leave room for a way back, we also leave room for hesitation, fear, anxiety, doubt, and resistance to creep in.

The challenge is to live full of faith, *passionate* faith. It's an invitation to discover a way to live . . . really live!

Regret

I hate regret. It gnaws on my gut like a bad taco. I chickened out once. I regret it. It's embarrassing.

I was back in Cuba for a second series of games against the Cuban national team. This time the president of the Cuban Basketball Federation, Tomas Herrera, hosted our team in his home city of Santiago de Cuba. While we were at his mother's house eating *arroz con pollo*, he said, "Palmer, now it's your turn to host us in Chicago."

He was right. He had rolled out the red carpet for my team in Havana, and in Santiago, he scheduled a week of great games in incredible venues. And now we needed to return the favor. So I said, "Sure, come next August! We will host you, and I will book a series of games against colleges around Illinois and Indiana."

What was I thinking? I was a college pastor, not an international basketball booking agent! On the flight back to Toronto I was already filling with fear, thinking, *This is never going to work. I'll never be able to book the colleges. I'll never have enough money for hotels and travel. I will fail and be shamed.*

I returned to Wheaton and managed to schedule four games with Christian colleges, but they only offered a few hundred dollars a game. I needed more games. I needed more money for the vans and hotel bills and restaurant tabs. So two months before the Cubans were to arrive, I backed out. I sent each coach a cowardly letter of cancellation, and one to Tomas in Cuba. He never bothered answering. One of the college coaches called and chewed me out for leaving him with no preseason game. I deserved the tongue-lashing.

I never believed for a minute I could pull off the tour. I never gave God a chance to show up and do something spectacular. Before I even had a chance to fail I sabotaged a once-in-a-lifetime opportunity by giving in to fear.

So that's it. I have no intriguing story of having my

Cuban friend Tomas in my home. I have no compelling accounts of Cuban basketball players, raised in communist agnosticism, praying to accept Christ. Nothing. Just failure from the fear of failure.

Your prophecies of failure will always come true, because you planned them. You enabled them and let them have their way with you. You fed them like a hungry dog. You doubted God. That cost you.

The bold Christ follower Paul warned us, "For a great and effective door has opened to me, and there are many adversaries."

There will be trials and trouble, difficulty, disappointment, and frustration . . . but those are not necessarily signs that you have walked through the wrong door. It's just that the life spent seeking after God requires courageous resolve.

When God Stops the River . . . Go!

Faith is the fuel of spiritual growth. You grow with each step of faith you take.

The passion stage is marked by a life of God-size faith. If you wonder who around you is maturing through this stage of faith, look at their life choices. Look at what they are doing for God. If they are attempting the absurd, the impossible, in the name of Christ, they are most likely the ones growing and moving toward a deep, thriving relationship with him.

I wasn't there, but I can promise you that with each step through the Jordan's dry riverbed the people's faith grew.

As a kid, when I saw Sunday school pictures of the Hebrew people crossing the Jordan, they were always in some kind of orderly procession, like a marching band in the Macy's Thanksgiving Day Parade. I don't think it was like that. I picture pushing and shoving and running and stepping over women and children—kind of like Black Friday at Walmart.

When God brought the raging river to a crashing halt, I think everybody knew it was time to bounce.

Sometimes the light turns green, and we turn to God and say, "What should I do now?" Sometimes the door swings open wide, and we refuse to step through, like we're not so sure God waits on the other side.

Don't make that mistake. The moments of opportunity pass quickly. There's a very good chance the door will not be open next week, or next month, or next year.

Playing it safe is never God's plan.

When the waters part, when the door opens, when the invitation comes—*go!*

If you have one foot on dry ground and one foot in the water, dive on in.

If you have one foot in the water and one foot in the boat, burn the boat.

Chapter 8

YOLO

My stomach turned as I watched CNN cover the Haiti earthquake. It had been four days since the devastating earthquake crushed a nation . . . and still no U.S. government personnel had started digging out survivors. We were still "assessing" the situation. We were still waiting for it to be "safe."

Unbelievable.

If people are trapped under mountains of concrete rubble, then there is no waiting! It's urgent. There is no assessing. The time to act is *now*! Hadn't our country learned anything from Katrina?

That was Saturday night. On Sunday morning, I stood up front at all three of our services at The Grove and said,

"We must do something! And if there's anything needed in Haiti right now, it is doctors and nurses. We need to send a medical team. If you can leave this week, please tell me immediately." People jumped at the invitation. By Monday night we had a team of ten.

Our team headed to the bleak Dominican port city of Barahona, where my friend Chris Clark, founder of Children of the Nations (COTN), had a clinic and told me they needed help with the wounded from Haiti.

Chris had reached the border town of Jimaní just days after the earthquake and found a dozen children with amputations lying under trees and on mattresses in the open, outside of an overcrowded hospital. They were still in their filthy clothes, ragged and torn from the rubble that fell on them. No one was treating them. He knew their wounds would soon be infected.

Fearing the worst, Chris began to urgently search for a way to evacuate the dozen children to the COTN clinic in Barahona, about a two-hour drive away. But the roads were bad. The rough ride would be torturous for the children. Chris knew they needed to be flown.

Chris waits for no one. He dialed his brother, who had been in the military, and said, "I need the name of the admiral leading the U.S. fleet that is on its way to Haiti." His brother, Bill, said he would do his best.

An hour later Bill had the admiral's name and email. Chris sent the admiral an urgent note, explaining he had a dozen kids who would die if they were not medevacked out. "Could you send your Black Hawks to fly them to Barahona?" Chris pleaded.

Chris hit *send* and went to bed, not really sure a U.S. admiral would take the time to read his email.

In the morning, he was back at the hospital when he noticed a man wearing fatigues walking the halls of the hospital, shouting, "Chris Clark. Does anyone here know a Chris Clark?"

Chris thought they were coming to take him away, so he had someone else go ask the man in uniform why he wanted Chris.

The man said he had a message from an admiral for Chris. Chris hurried over.

The first thing the man in uniform asked Chris was, "Who do you know in the White House?"

"No one," Chris answered, a bit surprised by the question. "Why?"

"Well, I don't know how you did it, then," the officer continued. "Because you have four Black Hawks on their way to take a dozen kids to your clinic in Barahona. Have them ready to go in two hours. And, by the way, I need the coordinates."

Chris couldn't believe it. He quickly dialed his wife in Seattle and said, "Get on Google Maps and find the coordinates of our clinic in Barahona."

"Your what?" She had no idea what he was talking about.

"My longitude and latitude!"

That didn't help, either.

Two hours later, the Black Hawks touched down.

In the meantime, just hours earlier, our team arrived at the small clinic in Barahona, ready to pitch in and help the small staff. As soon as The Grove team unpacked, Dr. Hodgson, our team leader, was told, "Prepare your medical team to receive postop children from Haiti. You'll need to meet them on the tarmac at the Barahona airport. They are being flown in on U.S. military Black Hawks."

The team hurriedly prepared for the kids and sped to the small airport. Along with the breeze blowing in off the Caribbean came the sound of chopper blades. Like a scene from *M*A*S*H*, the Black Hawks floated over the Sierra de Baoruco mountains that divide the Dominican Republic from Haiti and toward our waiting team on the runway.

With blades still churning, our team of doctors and nurses and EMTs eased the wounded children out the chopper doors and onto stretchers, carrying them through the gusting turbulence to a waiting squad of multicolored minivans that would temporarily serve as ambulances.

At the clinic our volunteers dumped bucket after bucket of muddy water as they gently sponged each child clean. The nurses exchanged their soiled and bloodied bandages for clean, white dressings and carefully pulled crisp, clean sheets over their frail bodies.

Though damaged, the children looked beautiful. It was an unforgettable experience.

What if Chris had believed somebody else would help the children? What if the people of The Grove had believed somebody else would be there to treat them? Nobody was. What if we joined in all the assessing and following of safety protocol and waiting? What if we believed cutting a check would be enough to meet the needs of the children in Haiti? On that day, no check in the world would have helped. What if we believed this disaster on a faraway island nation was somebody else's problem? Then a dozen desperate children would have continued to lie on filthy mattresses under trees by a dirt field.

Carpe Diem

To live with passionate faith is to live with more urgency.

I think procrastinators irritated Jesus.

In one incident John records, several men approached Him, saying, "We will follow You!" His response was, "Let's do it." But He knew they were groupies.

To one, He said, "Are you ready to rough it? We're not staying in the best inns, you know." He knew this guy wanted the circumstances to be perfect before he would go. It's not like that for the Christ follower.

To the second, who had an excuse about work, Jesus

bluntly answered, "First things first. Your business is life, not death. And life is urgent." In other words, eternal things matter most. Get busy with that. You'll always have work and the excuse of work and the excuse of needing more money. But now is the time; the kingdom work is desperately urgent. Exponentially more urgent than what is worrying you right now.

The third man had some flimsy words about needing to make sure everything at home was squared away . . . then he could fully commit to giving his life away for Christ. Jesus said, "No procrastination. No backward looks. You can't put God's kingdom off till tomorrow. Seize the day."

And that's it, isn't it? Carpe diem—seize the day. Your time to act is now. The day when you must give your life to changing this world for God is *today*!

We play it too safe. We have an anesthetized Christianity.

God invites you to leave the safe confines of your place in the pew and live the daring life He has for you.

Maybe it's time for a new career or a change in ministry. Time to finish the degree. Time to get on a plane.

Wake up your soul. Enough TV, enough shopping and golf just to fill your weekends. You are bright and intelligent and filled with potential . . . but you will die with all the possibilities on the inside if you don't *get up and get out*.

My twin brother, Paul, has a great saying: "You will always regret the things you do not do." I think he's right.

That's why I caved and bought tickets to the World Cup in Brazil for me and three of my sons to travel with Paul and his sons.

A few years ago, I had hounded my longtime friend Scott, whom I had grown up with in Liberia, to come bolster the soccer team of college students I was leading to Costa Rica, then travel on to Cuba with our band. He finally agreed to do the ten days in Costa Rica, but he said there was no way he could miss another week of work for Cuba.

When I stayed at Scott's house in Huntington Beach recently, he said, "Palmer, one of my greatest life regrets is not going to Cuba with you. I have no idea why I thought missing another week of work was such a big deal."

You see, the opportunities God gives us rarely come twice. The door swings wide open, but it always shuts.

I think that's why this time when I urged Scott to join us for the World Cup in Brazil, he didn't hesitate, and he brought his son.

YOLO—that's what my sons say when their parents try to say no to something daring—you only live once!

Usually these opportunities from God are much more local—where you live. A couple of my favorite examples come from Melissa and Gayleen.

Melissa loves babies and moms. Particularly neglected single moms. When she hears of a young single mom who's having a baby in our town, she finds out what she needs most. It's usually a stroller or a car seat, a high chair or baby clothes. Then she gets on Facebook and Twitter and tells everyone what the new mom needs. Melissa knows no one throws those kinds of things away, even when they're fifty and their babies are in college. Melissa says she usually finds everything the single mother needs in a day through her community's generosity.

Gayleen has a heart for strippers. She says they are more lonely and scarred than most people realize. So she cooks big warm meals, goes to the strip clubs at dinnertime, and sets a table in their break room. As the girls scarf down her savory dinner, she listens to their troubled stories. Gayleen tells them she cares, and God cares and He has a beautiful future for them.

Sometimes the girls quit stripping to start a new life and they come to our church. The strip club bosses get angry and kick Gayleen out, but they always end up inviting her back because the girls are hungry . . . for love.

I love how Melissa and Gayleen are living everyday justice as Jesus did.

Go Ahead and Jump

Here's how I picture it: when the Christ-follower Peter saw Jesus on the water walking toward him, I don't think he stepped over the side of the boat. I think he jumped. He seems like a jumper.

After speaking at a conference in San Diego, I dropped in on my son, who was a junior at Point Loma Nazarene University. He had been expecting me. "Okay, the guys are already waiting for us at Sunset Cliffs. Change quick; we're going cliff jumping."

"Huh?"

"Yeah. Remember? I told you I've been doing gainers off the thirty-foot-high ledge at Sunset Cliffs. I wanted to show you. Plus, I told all the guys you were going to do a gainer, too."

"What?"

I went ahead and changed into my swimsuit, not really sure where all this was leading.

We parked across the road from the cliffs, and sure enough half a dozen of his college buddies were waiting to watch *us* jump.

Ripping off his shirt, Byron sprinted for the edge of the thirty-foot-high cliff, jumped, leaned back, and pulled off a perfect full gainer: a forward-facing backward somersault.

Byron's friends, along with a crowd of almost fifty people, cheered wildly. Everyone else only jumped feetfirst, like kids off the high dive at the YMCA.

As we waited for him to climb back up, bystanders began sharing horror stories. "Man, I was here yesterday," one local said, "and a girl jumped off, but she got all crooked in the air. Dude, when she landed her thigh split open like a cantaloupe hitting the asphalt. Her friends carried her off bleeding!"

"Yeah, man," another chimed in. "I was here last week, and some crazy dude tried a cartwheel off here and the water busted his leg open just like that!"

As Bryon made his way back up to the cliff 's ledge, still soaking wet and full of adrenaline, he blurted, "Okay, Dad, your turn!"

"Seriously?"

"I told all the guys you taught me how to do a gainer and that you're going to show them yourself." He smiled.

"When did I ever teach you how to do a gainer like that?"

"Off our diving board at our pool back home."

"Are you nuts? That's a foot and a half off the water; this is more than thirty feet!"

"Well, Dad, you can't let the guys down now. They all came to watch you. YOLO!"

I handed him my iPhone and said, "Video it." At least we would have footage of my last moments on earth. I sprinted toward the edge, jumped, leaned back . . . and prayed. Really, it was going to be sheer luck if I landed on my feet. The odds of overrotating and landing flat on my back or underrotating and slapping the fire out of my stomach were both far better odds than doing a complete rotation and landing feetfirst.

Splash!

Stink, the water was cold. With all the worrying about dying, I hadn't even thought about how icy the Pacific is in September. But I was alive, and that felt really good. By some miracle I had landed feetfirst. You can watch it on my YouTube channel![1]

It's one of my favorite father-son moments. Byron said it was ridiculous.

Your best moments in life will never happen until you jump.

I honestly believe there is a direct connection between great leaps of faith and a deep, intimate, thriving relationship with God.

When Byron was two, I loved the way he greeted me when I came home. He was usually on our long sectional watching *Teletubbies* and would always do the same thing when I walked through the door. He would yell, "Dad!" then sprint the length of the couch and launch off the armrest . . . knowing I would drop whatever was in my hands (books, laptop, coffee mug) and catch him in my arms before he landed hard on the floor.

Maybe that's the kind of leap we all need to take with God. He'll be there. He'll catch you.

That's why I said I believe Peter jumped over the side of the boat.

He knew the Christ would catch him.

He knew if he was really going to live, he had to jump. Stop waiting.

Carpe diem. YOLO.

Go ahead and . . .

Jump.

Part 2

Authentic Faith:
The Longing for Authenticity

James Fowler's fifth stage of spiritual development, *authentic faith*, is marked by a deep, genuine connectedness to God. This is when we mature to the point that we step beyond the confines of mere faith practices and truly embody our faith in an integrated way.

Authentic faith describes a willingness to explore new ideas and integrate faith traditions other than our own. It celebrates the vastness of God and the limitless possibilities He has for life with Him and expressions of worship of Him.

People at this stage recognize the possibility that some past worship traditions and traditional attitudes are better left in the past and could have been wrong, and that new expressions of worship and oneness are possible. They acknowledge that in some ways we have made idols of our own Christian traditions and that many expressions of worship, over time, can be corrupted and need to be evaluated, challenged, and corrected.

The mark of people who reach this stage of faith is inclusiveness, the willingness to accept mystery and paradox—such as the kingdom of God being both *now* and *not yet*. They stop the dogmatic insistence that their position is the only right one and others are categorically wrong. They embrace wonder and—most important—the *other*.

Together let's explore the dynamics of *authentic spirituality*: embrace inclusion, increase participation, decrease institutionalism, and show more grace—with less shaming.

#No Filter

It was nearing midnight when the high school dean called, asking that I come pick up my son and niece. There had been alcohol on their homecoming party bus.

Arriving at the school, I was given the full story. A boy had sneaked alcohol onto the bus and shared it with a few friends. When the driver noticed what was going on, he headed back to school, where the boy with the bootleg in the brown bag bolted out the bus door, scaled the school wall, and ran into the cornfields.

After my son and niece got in the car I snapped, "Why'd

you stay on the bus? Did you know he had alcohol? Why didn't you call me to come get you?"

"We had no idea he had alcohol," they answered sheepishly. "We didn't know we should call you."

I still felt angry.

When we got home I sat and tried to calm down. Why was I so mad? They had done nothing wrong. Why did I feel all this tension over something that was out of their control? They were just on a bus with thirty other kids. Then I realized the source of my anger. I was afraid. Afraid someone at church would find out the pastor's son was on the booze bus. Afraid my reputation would be tarnished. Afraid church people would think less of me or criticize me.

It was all so ridiculous.

Later that night, I woke them up to apologize.

I decided that night I would quit trying to raise the perfect family.

Because that's an impossible standard. Anyone who acts that way is only pretending, and everybody knows. If I kept acting like I had the perfect family, I would be a fake.

It was Christmastime, and we were living deep in the Liberian bush, two hundred miles from the capital city, and I needed a gift for my wife, Veronica. I was perusing the local market hoping to find something, anything that would work as a Christmas gift when I saw one young vendor selling Chiclets gum, cigarettes, and . . . Rolex watches! I was like, "Bingo, that's a great gift!" Plus, he only wanted twenty-five dollars.

I wrapped it with care and put it under our two-foot-high plastic fir. On Christmas morning, I handed it to Veronica with pride, but when she opened it her face turned from joy to horror as she blurted, "It's a fake!" while flinging the watch across the room.

Fail.

I'm not sure what tipped her off so quickly. Could have been the featherlight weight of the watch. Could have been the big ticking motion, rather than a real Rolex's perpetual motion. Could have been the fact that she knew we did not have five thousand dollars to spend on a watch. Didn't matter how she knew, she wanted nothing to do with a fake.

We are all turned off by fakes. We don't care to be around others who pretend to be people they are not.

Conversely, we are drawn to those who are real, genuine.

People are attracted to authenticity. Everybody wants the real you and a real church. Nobody wants to follow an act.

But what does it actually mean to be authentic?

In recent years, a new field of psychological study has emerged: the study of authenticity. And the timing is right, because this next generation is obsessed with who and what is authentic.

In the past, experts in the field were hesitant to study authenticity; the trait seemed too nebulous, too subjective.

Yet the more that is learned about the human quality of being genuine, the more psychologists have realized it is a central quality of the human personality.

Some define authenticity as being true to oneself; the word *authentic* is derived from the Greek *authentikos*, meaning to have full control over or power over. So to use the word in a personal context, it refers to having control or power over oneself versus allowing social influences to have power over who one is.

Our natural tendency is to allow outside factors—for example, peer pressure—to influence what we value or how we behave. The authentic person, however, is willing to live free, for the most part, of these outside influences and be true to their own desires, their true self.

Perhaps it's our social-media-saturated world that has caused this next generation to be drawn toward authenticity.

They have been raised in a plastic culture of digital profiles. They crop, enhance, and filter their posts and profiles to only show them at their best. They compete with "friends" to be more interesting than everyone else, better looking than they really are. It's an edited life.

But that kind of digitally engineered profile—that kind of life—cannot be sustained. It's exhausting, and it's as fake as catfishing—the use of false identities fabricated on the Web.

I think that is why this next generation is demanding authenticity of each other . . . and of their faith.

"Authenticity."

That was Brad Lomenick's poignant answer when we served together on a conference panel titled "Capturing the Millennial Mind," and Brad was asked, "What do millennials desire most?"

I would put Brad at the top of the list of experts on millennials. For the past twelve years, he has led Catalyst, a church leaders' conference that has captivated millennials more than any other similar movement. He knows their pulse; he hears their heartbeat. I would listen to Brad.

Ironically, the title of the panel itself that Brad and I were on together illustrated the evangelical problem of focusing in on the wrong thing. What we should be asking is, how do we capture the millennial soul?

The future church does not want to be sold a product. They want authentic, organic Christianity. They sniff out imposters from miles away. If they think you are manipulating them or trying to "reach" them, they will run.

They are not so concerned with how right Christians are as much as they long for a genuine faith that walks out the truth of Jesus' teachings, that has a heart for justice and compassion, something with legs. They are not looking for intellectual battles or political fights. They want to live simply, act justly, love mercy, and walk humbly with God.

Recently, my millennial son climbed into the car to join us for dinner out, wearing a faded, floral-print shirt. "Where'd you get that?" I wondered out loud.

"Gramps left it."

My parents, his grandparents, had been visiting, and I guess my eightysomething-year-old dad had left an old, threadbare shirt in the closet. My son considered it just right for a Friday-night dinner out.

Nice.

I think every generation has its positive qualities and negative qualities. One admirable attribute I see in this next generation is their desire for authenticity. In fact, they have a near obsession with it.

Though difficult to define, the contemporary concept of authenticity is based primarily on that which is *vintage* and the idea of *austerity*. If products, ideas, or behaviors are *vintage,* more than several decades old, they are perceived to be more authentic—since they originated from a culture less corrupted by commercialization.

Authenticity is also closely connected to the idea of frugality today. The more simple something is—like a fixed-gear bike—the better.

So demanufactured versions of products have appeal over those that have been corrupted by our commoditized, consumer culture. They want raw and whole. They want organically grown grains, single-source dairy, and gourmet coffee. They disdain mass-produced, fake anything, office cubicles, and shampooing . . . yep, there's a no-shampooing movement. And if they do use soap, they want it artisanal and environmentally friendly.

These same kinds of values seep into their quest for God.

In the aughts (2000–2010), the church went hard after Generation X with concert-dark and loud auditoriums. They pumped in fog that made the light show vibrant for our Sunday-night Gen-X services . . . or even on Sunday mornings. Churches built expansive stages with enormous projection screens and hired production managers.

That was a decade ago. The next-generation Christian has grown tired of the show. They want something real. They want a church and worship that is more raw, less commercialized. Grassroots, not plastic.

I point out these things not because millennials get life right and the rest have it wrong. After all, much of the millennial culture's anticommercialism today is a rebirth of the Beat culture's antimaterialism. But we should always pay attention to what the current generation is asking us to change. And although I keep hearing pastors and church leaders ask how do we reach the next generation, I need to be blunt. It's time to change our old way of doing church and representing Jesus Christ. The political structures of how our churches are led ("governed") need to be dismantled, the excess needs to be replaced with austerity, and the dispassion toward injustice needs to end. Why? Not because the millennial needs to be reached—but because they can remind us that Jesus told us so.

Jesus spoke frequently of the spiritually disingenuous. The targets of His frustration were often the Jewish religious leaders, the Pharisees and the Sadducees. They were like bright plastic on the outside, Jesus said, but rotting on the inside. Their religion was a show of sorts, little more than an exercise in dramatic pageantry.

What Jesus seemed to desire most was a deeply heartfelt pursuit of God, like the man who beat his chest when he prayed honestly about his many sins.

Shows are for shallow spirituality.

God simply wants people who will follow Him with relentless, genuine passion. He's not so concerned with the performances and polished programming.

It was the religiously raw who seemed to interest Jesus the most: the woman in tears crawling to Him on her knees, the schemer hiding high in a tree.

Ancient Worship Today

I love it when people leaving our worship experience stop to say things like, "I enjoyed mass this morning." I never correct them and say, "We call it 'worship service' here, not mass."

We have this beautiful, eclectic mix of people from all kinds of faith traditions. And I think one of the reasons people who grew up going to mass feel comfortable is because we include ancient worship in our practice today.

But it's not just for those who grew up with it. In the midst of the next generation's mass exodus from the church, some churches are seeing a return of young adults who are seeking a more liturgical worship experience.

We are starting to crave the deepness of vintage worship—practices like liturgy and communion. In our electronic world of digital Facebook friends and Evites, superficiality permeates life. When the worshippers of today gather, they want something meaningful. So they are reaching back and giving new life to traditional practices such as *lectio divina* and responsive readings.

We acknowledge this desire at The Grove when we ask people to leave their seats to take communion. Our tables with the bread and cup are spread around the room, sometimes even in the middle of the room. On some Sundays we invite people to kneel as they take the Eucharist. We use actual flats of pita and Jewish matzo crackers that people dip in the chalice. I feel there's something powerful when a person must walk down an aisle or to the middle of the room to participate in remembering the death and resurrection of the Christ.

I understand why some churches stopped the liturgy and traditional customs; they had become rote and a kind of ritual. But we are rediscovering the original heart behind those ancient practices, finding that people thrive on the depth of language and the soulfulness of liturgy. They want to read creed together, recite holy texts, and have meaningful prayer.

They crave reverent moments, authentic spirituality, and sacred space. They want to feel the wooden pew, touch the bread, and smell the candles. Today we are not impressed by the artificial sounds of a Sanyo keyboard synthesizer; we would rather hear crisp notes rise from the strings of the violin.

In a surprising turn for the good, many churches are trading contemporary styles of worship for more ancient practices, to meet this renewed desire for something more sacramental.

In the same way we crave the authentic, rugged simplicity of a manual, upright typewriter, we crave a faith that is aged and austere and real. People want to reach back—not to 1970, but further back, like 1570—to touch the ancientness of a faith that has been with us for two thousand years.

In a land of cheap fast food, a new sacramental craving is growing. In the midst of our overcommercialized consumer culture, people hunger for a faith with substance, a faith with depth and history. This longing for the sacred runs deep in every soul. And so this next-generation Christian is drawn to churches and worship that connect them with a faith that is ancient, sacred, and authentic.

Chapter 9

RACISM AND THE REAL YOU

After a coup d'état rocked Liberia, my home growing up, our family returned to America for ten months. My twin brother, Paul, and I were signed up for eleventh grade at a "Christian" academy . . . in Mississippi. That school year was surreal. We went from high school in Monrovia, where more than half our friends were African, to a private Christian school without a single person of color. We were quintessential misfits, our friendships strained at best. They called us Yankees—which made no sense, because I thought I was from Africa.

Charles invited Paul over to his house one afternoon to throw knives—did I mention we were in Mississippi? While futilely trying to get a hunting knife to stick in a pine tree from twenty feet, Charles casually asked, "So Paul, when you were in Africa, did you ever eat with a black person?"

"Yeah, all the time," Paul answered. "Why do you ask?"

"Because I never have," Charles answered, then paused. "But my grandfather had breakfast with a black person."

I share this because I knew Charles, too. And even though Charles was raised with a bias, I do not believe he was a racist.

The trouble is, Charles was raised in a racialized society.

I do not believe most Christians are racists. The problem is we still live in a divided society. Culturally we are not one. We have been divided into schools and workplaces and neighborhoods and . . . churches.

To make things worse, most of us were raised in a swamp of stereotypes. Stereotyping goes hand in hand with racism. Somewhere deep under the skin—at the soul level—we form biases as a result of our environment. It could be toward Asians, Hispanics, African Americans, or Caucasians. I challenge you to look deep within and work to put your finger on the source of your own biases, as small as they may seem.

I would ask, were your prejudices influenced by a family member, a school friend, a coworker, a newscaster or talk show host, an authority figure? Because the you God made was not born with these mind-sets. Bigotry is a learned behavior shaped by countless external influences.

Think about the authentic you, the *you* you know God made. The you who actually cares about the immigrant, enjoys hanging out with kids of other races at your school, appreciates the artistry, food, and culture of another group. However, this part of you is often dormant. We sense we will be mocked and ridiculed by those like us, who openly brandish their prejudices. So we mimic their behavior and biases. We fail to embrace, love, or move toward the other.

We can change this.

We can change.

Justice Precedes Reconciliation

In the eighties and nineties, countless books, videos, and speeches addressed racial reconciliation. Seminars and conferences were held. Little has changed.

I hear quite a bit of talk about reconciliation in the Christian community. Here's what I think: We need to slow down, because reconciliation cannot be realized until we first pursue justice.

I applaud the efforts of individuals and churches and Christian leaders to ask for forgiveness, to promote diversity in their congregations, hire staff of different races, and even personally grow cross-racial friendships. My point, however, is that all of this rings hollow if we are not first pursuing justice.

To seek reconciliation for wrongs of generations past yet do little or nothing to stop the injustice all around today is glib.

Let's say a group of white southern pastors gather with pastors of local African American churches to apologize for their denomination's apathy and silence during the civil rights movement of the 1960s. The white pastors give speeches of remorse and make promises to promote greater diversity in their churches. Then all the pastors have lunch together.

This is all good and beautiful.

But then what if the next day an African American teen is mistakenly identified as a criminal, shot, and killed? And the pastors of the African American churches gather with the people of their community to march the streets of their city, carrying placards that read Black Lives Matter, No Justice No Peace . . . while all the while the white pastors stay home and watch their new friends on the evening news.

Do you see why all the talk of reconciliation begins to feel fake—inauthentic—if we are not crying out for justice with them, if we do not march in solidarity with our neighbors? If we do not cry with the mothers of their dead teenagers when they cry?

True reconciliation begins by walking with the oppressed. We can only honestly ask for reconciliation after we have pursued justice.

Justice is a prerequisite to reconciliation.

I like the way multicultural speaker and writer Austin Channing puts it: "Reconciliation requires far more than hugs, small talk, and coffee dates. Being nice is, well . . . nice, but it is not reconciliation. Reconciliation is what we do as we listen to hard truths from the marginalized among us. . . . Drinking in the words. Sitting in the pain. Committing to understanding. Committing to doing better."[1]

The Body Is Not One

The call to be one is a central theme of the New Testament church. Paul the Apostle writes, "There is no longer Jew or Gentile, slave or free, male and female. For you are all one in Christ Jesus."[2]

How can we be real with God when we are not real with our neighbor?

We talk of inviting God into our hearts, but have yet to invite our neighbor into our home, we have yet to invite our landscaper into our church sanctuary.

Where did it all go wrong? I think I know: we have separated our relationship with God from our relationship with people. We have made our spirituality so inner, so personal, so much about our mind and soul, that we have ignored

Jesus' call to love our neighbor. That part of the gospel we don't talk about so much, as though loving our neighbor is a nice thing to tack onto our spirituality.

I would argue that how we treat and love our neighbor is at the very core of what it means to be an authentic follower of Jesus Christ. Because until we are one with our neighbor, with our community, with the other, with the least and the last we can never be one with God.

We hear it said that Sunday is the most divided day in America. I've seen it. It's sad. But you and I can change that.

For the past century Christians have filled mission stations with missionaries in faraway lands. We send checks and crates of supplies to the *mission field* and the *missionaries,* all the while living and worshipping in segregation. We like missions, we don't like living on mission. People will cut a check for the children in Africa or send a team to dig a well in Asia, but few are actually willing to live on mission every day. We want to preach the good news; we are not so interested in being the good news. We don't mind delivering it from a distance. What we struggle with is sharing a pew, sharing a meal, sharing a living room on a Sunday afternoon when the football game plays on TV.

The trouble is, when we fail to live on mission six days of the week, then on Sundays we simply become actors on a stage. Because our performance at church does not match the life we live every day.

The inauthenticity is glaring.

Close the Distance, Embrace the Other

Racism is when prejudice is pointed toward a particular race, ethnicity, or nationality. Racism happens when we speak negatively, act unfairly, or think the worst about a person or people based solely on the color of their skin or country of origin.

The good news is racial attitudes can change.

It begins with four fundamental commitments:

We Will Include You

When we develop friendship with people of other races and ethnicities, the walls begin to crumble. Researchers say it is nearly impossible to retain bigoted attitudes when you have a close friend in that group. A friendship increases identification and empathy with people different from you. And most important, your friendship becomes *part of who you are.*

We Will Celebrate Your Presence

When people of diverse ethnicity join us in worship, let's begin celebrating our differences. And this cannot be only in our place of formal worship; let's make this the norm in our living rooms and our backyard barbecues.

We Will Walk with You

If our friendships with people of other races are genuine, then in their moments of great need or sorrow we will not remain at a distance. We will go to them, be one with them, walk with them.

We Will Stand Up for You

You have heard the snide, bigoted comments at work, you have heard the stereotyping among friends. It's time to speak up. It's time for you to put a stop to the discrimination when it happens.

Silence is a form of consent.

The justice prophet Isaiah says, "The watchmen are blind. They are all dumb dogs, they cannot bark. They are sleeping."[3]

Instead, become a deliberate presence for racial oneness in your neighborhood, in your workplace, in your church.

It's Time to Worship as One

John Perkins was only sixteen when his twenty-five-year-old brother, who had just returned from fighting in World War II, was shot. The marshal said he was talking too loudly in the theater. As he was being dragged from the movie house in front of his girlfriend he protested ever so slightly, but that was enough for the Mississippi marshal to pull out his pistol and shoot him in the head.

John's brother was dead. That's why John left Mississippi and vowed never to return.

When he left Mississippi, he left the church. Christianity, in his opinion, was the religion of the white man. And John wanted nothing to do with following the white man. The kind of church John knew in rural Mississippi was segregated. The white people had their church and the black were supposed to have their own. If the black people and white people did mix in church, the black were to sit upstairs in the balcony. Out of sight and out of mind.

So John left his bootlegging, rural Mississippi town and moved as far away as possible, geographically and ideologically—to California. He married Vera Mae and had a son named Spencer. When Spencer entered preschool and gave his life to God, John says he could not believe the striking changes he saw God work in Spencer's life. "I could see something was developing in him that was beautiful, something I knew nothing about. I'd had no real experience before of seeing Christianity at work like that in a person's life—at work in a way that was beautiful. . . and good."[4]

I've had the privilege of getting to know Dr. Perkins, who now has thirteen honorary doctorates from Wheaton College, Belhaven University, and Taylor University, to name a few. Today he is a minister, civil right activist, writer, Bible teacher, philosopher, community developer, and a voice crying out for justice and equality. And even better, he is voice calling for the church to be one.

It's time for every church in our country to throw its doors open wide.

We cannot do this passively. We must actively include the *other* in our leadership, in our pastoral roles, in our living room small groups. Everything from our websites to our front-door greeters must authentically represent the diversity of people God put on planet earth.

The days of *us* versus *them* are over. It's not like that in the next church—the churches that best reflect Jesus. It's *we*.

They say in the early fifties when Billy Graham first began holding tent crusades, his ushers put up ropes to separate blacks from whites. Graham himself walked through the tent, taking down the ropes that divide. Which led him to famously say, "The ground at the foot of the cross is level."

We need to focus on this again. Look around at your life, at your church. What barriers divide you and your neighbor or coworker? In what ways does your church put up walls between people? How are affluent people—the big givers—treated with preference to those on welfare?

Take them down. Dismantle them. Embrace diversity. Develop meaningful friendships with those outside your comfort zone. Lead the way in your personal life and in your church life.

And take the first step—do justice. Walking with the oppressed is a giant step toward spiritual maturity. The walls you allow between you and the other also become barriers to spiritual development. They keep us halfway. They keep you on the shallow side of spirituality.

So . . .

Walk as one—pursue justice.

Do life as one—build relationships.

Worship as one—throw the church doors open wide.

And you will grow.

Acknowledge, Confess, Change

Of all the places in the world where people gather, the church has to be a place where racial and ethnic diversity is celebrated and promoted. Where the walls that divide come down. Where authentic acceptance and love dominate. Because the church is at its best and reflects God's best when we worship him with people of every ethnicity, race, nationality, and color.

Where do we begin? I have three suggestions:

Acknowledge *We Have a Problem*

Last summer when I traveled to Brazil with three of my sons for the World Cup, a seminary professor and family friend, Elias, insisted we stay with his parents. They treated us like family.

Unfortunately, that's not how Elias had been treated when he moved from South America to the American South. His children particularly felt ostracized at school.

One afternoon his youngest daughter came home visibly upset. "Dad! Is Pelé black?" she blurted, wondering about Brazil's legendary football king.

"Why are you asking?" Elias asked in return.

"Because the kids at school keep saying Pelé is black!"

"Well, what did you say he was?" Elias asked.

"I just said Pelé is Brazilian!"

"Of course he is!" Elias exclaimed, surprised by the brilliance of his small daughter.

She did not think of Pelé as brown or white or black, or any other skin tone. He's Brazilian, that's it.

And that's how Elias says they see life in Brazil. Brazil is comprised of this heavenly mosaic of color from practically every corner of the globe. There are Brazilians of Portuguese descent, African descent, German descent, and of course indigenous South American descent . . . even a large population in São Paulo is of Japanese descent. When we walked out on the beach in Natal it was like arriving at the United Nations. It was beautiful, like heaven.

Elias explains, "In Brazil, we don't think in terms of race and ethnicity . . . we are all simply Brazilian."

I wish the rest of the world lived like that. I wish in our country we lived like that. We don't.

Instead we deny and dismiss the problem, which only makes it worse.

All the angry newscasters and talk show hosts, for example, who dismiss the abusive manhandling of a Texas African American teenage girl in a swimsuit only worsens the problem. Or when they deny the abusive treatment of a Baltimore teen who died in a van. Or refute the choking death of a New York cigarette vendor. Or defend the symbols of racism and slavery that fly high over statehouses. Or dismiss the shooting death of nine African American worshippers in church as *mental insanity*—rather than the racism that it is—exacerbates the problem.

Most Christians and churches do not intentionally put up walls between races; it's just that the society we live in has created divisions and barriers. But we cannot begin to make change or heal until we admit this problem is real. A problem cannot be dealt with unless we acknowledge its presence.

Then the walls can come down.

Then we can begin to heal.

Then one day soon we will live as one.

Confess *Your Role*

Confession creates all kinds of discomfort. We resist admitting our wrongs.

My challenge to you is to confess that in some small way you—I—have contributed to the problem.

If we are honest, to a degree we have all failed at some time, in some way, to love or accept or include. I ask you today to look deep inside and confess your own biases against other people, other races, other nationalities or ethnicities. Confess the stereotypes you have formed, the words you have spoken under your breath, the thoughts you have harbored. The problem is, stereotyping leads to racism. Stereotyping is when an individual is grouped into negative and derogatory categories. When this happens, stereotyping contorts into racism.

And confess your apathy and silence. Few of us have said, *Enough*. Too few have intervened or defended the cause of the marginalized. The people of God can do better.

Commit *to Change*

Commit to new attitudes and actions.

Jesus said there is nothing exceptional in loving people who are like you. The real work comes in accepting, including, befriending, and embracing those who are not like you.[5]

Our natural tendency is to find affinity with those who

are like us. That's easy. That comes naturally. My invitation to you is to find affinity with the dissimilar.

This is where you put your beliefs into practice. Will you sit by them and with them? Walk with them and for them? Eat out together, vacation together, laugh together? Live life as one?

We are good at charity, we are not so good at unity.

There is a monumental difference between feeding people and having a meal with people. When we only feed people, we keep them at arm's length. I think that's why we would rather send checks and fill food pantries than sit at a dining room table as one.

Deep, personal relationships are the best foundation for racial reconciliation.

Not long ago my cousin Chase was in a southern state for work. He and a friend stopped at a restaurant off the freeway for lunch. They sat there, he said, for over an hour waiting to be served. No one ever came. Then it dawned on him: "No one is serving us because my friend is African American!"

Chase is from Northern California, where he says people don't think anything about sharing a meal with someone of another race. In fact, his own uncle is African American. But in some places in this country—shockingly—people are still not eating as one.

Chase said they just got up and left.

You and I need to start changing things. Because *au-*

thentic faith can only be realized when we stop focusing on the difference between "them" and "us," when we break down the barriers and take down the ropes that divide.

My challenge to you is to commit to new attitudes and actions. Commit to new friendships. Commit to live as one.

When we share a meal, we share stories, we share recipes, we share dreams. We talk and laugh and sometimes cry. We double-dip and spill drinks. And best of all, we live life together—as one.

Chapter 10

PARTICIPATION PROMOTES AUTHENTICITY

I had been away from the pastorate for two years teaching at a Christian university and was missing it. I felt ready to jump back in, so I began sending my résumé around and called several friends to let them know I was looking. When I talked to my close friend Bret, his immediate response was, "You have to church-plant, Palmer. That's what you need to do!" His enthusiasm was obvious.

I just laughed. "No way, Bret. Church-planting is for losers who can't find a job after seminary."

"Palmer, you don't understand," Bret said. "The sharpest guys in the country are church-planting. Here's the best part: you get the opportunity to grow the church you've always dreamed of."

His last sentence got me. I began to imagine church the way I always dreamed it could be—authentic and real and genuine, without all the denominational baggage that can suffocate so many in the bondage of mere traditionalism and polity for the sake of polity—and it was beautiful and exhilarating.

And then I stopped dreaming about planting a church and started doing it.

It was raw and unpolished. We had no mother ship, no megachurch, no national church-planting agency behind us. It was simple, genuine, authentic. It was good, and I sensed God was doing something unique and exceptional.

As our new church in Arizona, The Grove, grew, we stumbled on an astonishing finding: *participation is powerful*. For me, the realization hit home on our second Barefoot Sunday, a day when we asked people to leave their shoes onstage and go home barefoot, so we could give our shoes away in Africa. After we took off our shoes, we invited everyone to step into pans of colored paint and walk over sheets of plywood to create community art. As the beige pine filled with brightly colored footprints, I began to sense the power of participation.

And art.

We displayed the footprint-covered plywood in our courtyard for a month—an art gallery of sorts—a reminder of everyone's commitment to take off their shoes and walk the holy ground of a broken world. That summer, more than one hundred of the barefoot who walked with painted feet stepped onto a plane that carried them an ocean away to walk on African soil.

Paul in the Bible was right: "How beautiful are the feet of those who bring good news!"[1]

Now we see the pattern clearly: the more people participate in the mission of the church, the more they grow, the more they flourish and the church thrives.

The more we invite people to participate in the worship experience, the more of God they absorb in their lives.

The more we ask them to participate in culture, the more they shape it.

The more we challenge them to participate in doing justice, the more passionately they live.

In decades past, it seemed the church was okay with creating spectators. People would watch and donate from a distance. But this next generation is different. They don't care to watch a show on Sunday morning. They will not stay on the sidelines of global change. They are not comfortable with dispassion or disengagement from culture. They do not want to leave the ministry and mission of the church to paid professionals or a department of the church. They want in.

They want to participate.

Because deep inside we all sense that participation is critical to authentic spirituality.

Mountain of Forgiveness

When I crested Mount Sinai and saw the Bedouins sitting by the fire, I knew I had carried the backpack full of sin to the right place.

Several weeks earlier, on an ordinary Sunday in March, I had talked about an outcast woman who found Jesus having dinner. Weeping and weighted by her sins—the Bible writer Luke says they were many—she fell at His feet and washed them with her tears. I spoke of how we all live heavy with sin, but it doesn't have to be that way, because her sins and our sins are left on a cross in Jerusalem.

That Sunday, we invited everyone who came to worship to write their most weighty sins on blue index cards. Then, as we worshipped, each person came to the front and nailed their card to a rugged wooden cross.

It was the first time we had asked people to participate like this. Walking an aisle, carrying their sins in hand, people would feel so vulnerable. I didn't know if even five people would make the walk.

We were wrong. A crowd formed around the cross, and the rugged wood quickly turned blue, covered with sins left behind.

When our services were over, a young woman pulled the cards off the cross, stuffed them into a bag, and handed them to me.

I hadn't planned this far ahead. What was I supposed to do now with a bag full of sin?

I carried them around in my satchel for days, not quite sure what to do. Should I just toss them into the trash? The recycle bin? But then I thought maybe we shouldn't recycle sin.

Two weeks later, packing for a trip to Egypt to climb Mount Sinai, I thought, *I'll take them with me.* I needed to be rid of the many sins.

I shoved the bag stuffed with blue cards into my backpack.

When we arrived in Egypt, we slept on the banks of the Nile, then the Red Sea. I thought about throwing the blue cards in, but that felt more like littering than confessing.

Finally, we reached Sinai and began our five-hour climb to the top of the mountain. The bag of sins was still in my backpack. On the ascent our guide casually mentioned, "The Hebrew people call this the Mountain of Forgiveness."

"They do?" I questioned. "Why?"

"Because after Moses destroyed the first Ten Commandments when he found the people worshipping a golden calf, he came back to the top of the mountain and pleaded with God to forgive them . . . and God did!"

Now I knew: the bag filled with many sins needed to stay behind on the Mountain of Forgiveness.

The sun was setting when we made the summit: a stone

chapel sat alone at the peak. Rounding the small building we found several Bedouins huddled around a fire, staying warm from the chill of the evening air.

I sat down next to them, then asked if I could burn a few things in their fire. Puzzled but gracious, they nodded, then watched quietly as I fueled their flames with the many sins. The papers smoldered, burned, and slowly drifted away in smoke and ash, forever lost in the night sky.

I waited a year before sharing that I had burned the many sins on the Mountain of Forgiveness. I waited until the Easter season when I taught about Peter's moment of denial and failure and, more important, about the fire Jesus stoked for Peter at daybreak. I talked of how, as they sat near the charcoal fire, Jesus forgave him and told him it was time to start again.

On that Sunday, once again, I invited all who carried guilt from past mistakes, all who carried shame, all who felt heavy with sin, to write their failure on a small piece of wood. Just outside the windows of our auditorium, we had fires burning. As we worshipped I said, "You can leave your many mistakes and failures here now; the fire burns for you." The room emptied, and our band played to abandoned seats—as people waited near the fire to burn their sins.

Participation is powerful.

Spectators

We live in a spectator culture. Football alone has more than a million spectators annually. Watching baseball is the national pastime. The average American, by the end of his or her life, will have spent nine years watching TV. (Sidenote: Studies now show that for every hour of TV viewing, your life expectancy is shortened by twenty-two minutes.)

My sons, in high school and college, never read the news; they watch it on Yahoo!, ESPN, and YouTube. They will huddle over an iPhone for an hour watching Vines, Plays of the Day, and Internet nonsense. My youngest son texted me last week when I was out of town: "Dad, can I buzz my head? I know how; I just watched a YouTube video."

We are watchers.

So it should be no surprise that our spectator culture has moved into the church and given us churches designed like movie theaters, "church TV," video venues, and satellite church.

Churches, like football teams, have Monday-morning quarterbacks who have spent a lifetime watching, never doing. Critiquing, never participating.

And churches, like football teams, need people who are willing to have some skin in the game—participants.

I have a friend who coaches in the NFL, so I've heard him talk about why teams want only their players and coaches on the sidelines. He's clearly agitated when he tells me about the well-dressed spectators management sometimes let slip onto the sideline. And how, during one humiliating loss, these spectators stood around laughing, chatting, and taking selfies. For the players and coaches, a career is on the line with each loss. But these spectators, he says, have no dog in the fight.

Does that describe us as followers, "fans," of Jesus Christ? "No dog in the fight?" I hope not.

When we lived in Los Angeles, I religiously watched Fred Roggin's *Sunday Night Sports*. With rapid, energetic analysis he jumped from sport to sport, highlight to highlight.

One of my favorite clips he showed was from a high school football game. A kid had broken a kickoff return and was headed for the end zone. He was sprinting down the sideline, when suddenly a player from the opposing team came flying off the sideline and laid him out. The kid on the sideline couldn't take it anymore. The bench was killing him. He was done being a spectator. The action was on the field.

My friend Frank Reich, a former NFL quarterback, says, "We all just want to be where the action is."

That's where your church needs you. Participating, not just watching.

Participatory Architecture

From my vantage point, much church architecture has become banal. In the Midwest, it looks like we've taken our architecture from shopping malls. On the West Coast, we've built dark movie-theater-style sanctuaries with stadium seating. Down south, we build massive brick structures with white Roman pillars out front. And in the Southwest, we use a lot of beige stucco.

Understand, there is nothing wrong or unbiblical about any of these kinds of buildings—architecture is like art, beauty is in the eye of the beholder. I simply think we can create worship spaces that promote greater authenticity and less production.

So when we started to design worship space for the future church, I called friends in the construction business to ask for names of architects, with one simple criterion: no church architects. I didn't want to put up another beige, stucco-covered, strip-mall-looking church.

My friend Wade told me to call Jack DeBartolo. After one phone conversation with Jack, before I had seen any of his work, I knew he was the right architect. He had just returned from doing a pro bono project in Liberia, building a school in the bush. He also taught part-time at Arizona State University and took students to places like Ethiopia to design and build orphanages. And, in our brief conversation, he offered to draw plans for the church we wanted to build in Haiti as well.

I told Jack we wanted to build in the round, something like a sprawling New Testament living room. I thought he would hate it. He loved it.

Descriptions of New Testament worship always seem to be characterized by participation. People came together to meet each other's needs; they prayed together and ate together and worshipped together. They came to participate—with God and in community.

It seems like we do pretty well at leading people to sing together on Sunday mornings, but that's about it. In most churches, little effort is made to create participants. So our goal in this new sacred space was to design a place of worship that would naturally invite people to participate.

Here are a few values that shaped our architecture.

Authentic Space

I knew there had to be a better way than to build another auditorium that forced hundreds of worshippers to look at each other's backs. So I sketched out a sacred space in the round.

Sitting in a circle, as opposed to sitting in rows that point in one direction, changes the dynamics of worship in several important ways:

In the round you see faces. When I walk into a crowded worship auditorium and all I see during the entire service is the backs of heads, I find it impersonal.

You also see others worship. You see the joy on people's faces. And sometimes the pain.

Sitting in the round also allows musicians and speakers to be at a more natural distance from the audience. In most large worship auditoriums, the rows of pews or seats go back at least one hundred feet, some stretching more than two hundred feet.

The problem is, the natural distance for sight and sound is only about sixty-five feet. So in auditoriums that stretch one hundred to two hundred feet deep, people in the back half of the room never see the facial expressions of those communicating.

To compensate, churches have introduced IMAG (image magnification), the camera and projection system that projects an image of the person on stage, sometimes ten times larger than life.

What most do not realize is that when you put an image on a screen, it changes the way the brain works—literally. Shane Hipps, author of *Flickering Pixels*, explained to me that when we watch images projected on a screen, the flickering pixels subconsciously affect our cognitive function. The rapidly blinking light leaves us relaxed and unresponsive, almost anesthetized.

Not long ago I spoke at a large Christian university. Nearly ten thousand students filled the auditorium. Just before going onstage, one of their staff pulled me aside to say, "Palmer, don't let it bother you that while you're speaking most of the students will not be looking at you. They tend to focus on the big screens. Even students sitting in the front row will look past you and at the screens. A lot of our guest speakers are really distracted when this happens."

I shrugged it off and didn't think much about it . . . until I was about ten minutes into my talk, and I realized that students sitting on the front row were not looking at me. It's not that they were checking their texts or falling asleep; they seemed to be staring off into space while I was trying to make eye contact. Finally, I turned to see what they were looking it. Me! Yes, I had forgotten; there was my huge mug on two big screens high behind me, to my right and left.

Is the use of giant screens wrong? I don't know about that. Very large churches have to bring people closer to the speaker somehow. But it creates distance of another kind.

Posture of Participation

Most of us don't think much about the furniture we sit on during worship, but posture in worship matters immensely.

The current trend in many new worship auditoriums has been to install rows of reclining seats. Cushioned seats that lean back pose several problems in worship. First, imagine trying to sing while lying in bed. You can't (not very well, at least). You can't project. You cannot fill your lungs with air.

But as with the screens, the chair itself also conveys a message. The cushioned, reclining seat tells your mind and body that you are there to watch, not participate. The theater seat subtly says, "You are here to be entertained; lean back and enjoy. You are an observer, not a participant."

Conversely, an upright seat (picture a wooden chair in a coffee shop) sends quite the opposite message. It tells you to lean in, participate. The chair at a bistro table, on another note, promotes conversation and interaction.

Straight-back, wood chairs also communicate this subtle message: "Don't get too comfortable. Your place in this world is not in here; it's out there. The local church is not the end; we are only the means God uses to send you out."

Natural Light

When Jack began to design our worship space, I told him we wanted daylight, natural light, which used to be the norm in church architecture. Not anymore. I told him we wanted to see the grove of trees in which our church sits—the very grove that inspired our church's name. I asked him if we could allow people to see the blue skies that make people sell their homes in Duluth and move to Arizona.

As it did to church architects centuries ago, it seemed fitting to want light from above to leak into our sacred space. It symbolizes our identity as people of the light—because Jesus came as the light of the world. Another compelling reason was that where there is no light, there is no color. So only when churches throw open the windows can we see the mosaic of people who fill our worship houses.

Worship Neighborhoods

We have also created *seating neighborhoods* to foster community and help people connect. To do this we've designed an auditorium that uses terraces at varying elevations and sizes and a variety of seating types to break up the room into about twenty seating sections (or *hoods*).

When this idea first came up, I drew floor plans on a legal pad to show our staff what I was envisioning. Paul Gunther, who grew up in Thailand before settling in Guatemala, blurted, "It's like rice paddies."

Sure!

So now we have a few bistro sections, where people sit around high tops in small groups, together. We also have several large, heavy wooden dining room tables that families, or a family of friends, can sit around and interact and worship. We've even incorporated a section of pews to keep us from forgetting that we have an ancient sacred tradition that spans centuries. And we do have a few couch sections—I think we should call that "neighborhood" Shalom, where all who are tired and need rest can come and be restored.

Obviously, The Grove isn't the first or only church to look at current church trends for new ways to help us reflect the

God we worship. Churches around the country are retrofitting and repurposing their worship spaces. My favorite is another church community's, in fact: Vintage Faith in Santa Cruz, California. In their worship space, the pastor, Dan Kimball, and his team have created sacred spaces for prayer, art, liturgy and poetry reading, and meditation. Everything about the room invites participation, and it's very much a sacred space.

The point isn't to compare churches. God inhabits the praises of his people, not the seats and stages we declare them from. So as you think about how you bring yourself to the worship service, you can help create a new kind of church, too, in the broader, more significant sense. A church where people participate in worship, in the mission of the church, and in filling their communities and this world with the beauty, compassion, generosity, and love of God.

This is no minor shift. It means going back to Scripture to reclaim the most biblical idea of spirituality—a spirituality that compels God's people to participate in His redemptive plan for this world: rescue exploited girls, compose music, repair blighted neighborhoods, plant gardens, hang mosquito nets, make art, care about immigrants, and share the good news of God's love.

Chapter 11

FROM INSTITUTIONAL TO AUTHENTIC

As I sat through the worship service I looked around at the eight hundred people in painful captivity. The preacher, perched high above his defeated audience, was wedged oddly in a podium loft, wearing a black velvety gown. As he pontificated about some obscure theological nuance, I wondered, is anyone listening? When he was finally done, the pipe organ droned as people mumbled words to a hymn of which they had long since wearied.

Making our way to the parking lot afterward, I asked my relative who regularly attended the church, "Why do people keep coming back? I don't get it. If this church was on the West Coast you wouldn't have ten people in the pews."

His answer was comically tragic: "The emperor has no clothes."

He was right. People kept coming because it was good to be seen at this church. It was good for the real-estate business, and the dental business, and the law business . . . plus, everyone felt smarter. The church was known for its intellectual fortitude, and simply being a member enhanced your reputation. So the audience dutifully obliged.

When a congregation is known more for its social status than for its resemblance to God, that's a problem.

I'm not breaking any news when I say the data overwhelmingly tells us that the current generation of young adults—the millennial—is disenfranchised with traditional, institutional forms of Christianity.

According to the Hartford Institute for Religion Research, 40 percent of Americans say they attend church weekly, but the truth is that number is more like 20 percent.[1] The United States boasts about 350,000 churches. Sadly, four thousand of them close every year, and only one thousand new churches replace them. It would seem difficult to contest the fact that church as we have known it in the West is dying.

The opulence of the polished megachurch, all the church politics, the dispassion toward injustice, and traditionalism divorced from substance has left a sour taste in the mouth of today's Christians. Meaningful spiritual development is not happening. Lives are not being transformed.

What is the problem?

Institutionalized

We've institutionalized God.

It's a very Western thing to put God in a matrix.

It's not a bad idea. I'm just not so sure God ever asked to be systematized.

As far back as I can remember, I was taught that greater knowledge equaled greater spirituality.

At least, that was my impression in Sunday school, when the kids who memorized verses each week had gold stars pasted next to their names. So we memorized Bible verses the way NFL quarterbacks memorize playbooks.

Of course, if we're going to know the Bible, it's a good idea to know how to find our way around it. And like vocab lists in Foreign Language 101, some things you just have to memorize. But for many, that becomes the sum total of their Christian experience: information transfer. We are told information will change people, so we pour as much into them as humanly possible. We preach, hold classes, write books about "systematic theology," and expect the academic excellence of a university undergrad.

In fact, knowledge itself is considered virtuous. Seasoned church planter and author Frank Viola calls it *liquid pedagogy*. "Contemporary theological learning is essentially cerebral. . . . We pry open people's heads, pour in a cup or two of information, and close them up again. They have the information, so we mistakenly conclude the job is complete. Contemporary theological teaching is data-transfer education."[2]

There are things we must learn. But *knowing* is not enough.

A casual reading of Jesus' famous parable of the Good Samaritan gives the impression the story is about kindness to strangers and helping others—which it is—but I wonder if Jesus meant for the story to be mostly about the other characters. The religious intellects of Jesus' day who walked around the wounded man; the ones who made spirituality primarily an intellectual experience, detached from the troubled world in which they lived.

Do you see Jesus' point, how overintellectualizing our faith can lead to dispassion? When we make the kingdom a cognitive experience it lets us off the hook, because faith, then, is only about *knowing* rather than *doing*.

Kingdoms on Street Corners

Institutions need buildings.

The New Testament church had no building. The temple is Old Testament theology.

Some say we have Constantine to blame for modern Christianity's obsession with buildings. As emperor, in 312 AD he commissioned the construction of churches throughout the empire. The gods and the Jews had temples; Constantine likely thought that if Christians had buildings as well, it would legitimize the new faith.

We still do this today. The moment we find a community anywhere in the world, our greatest priority seems to be to build them a church. As though the absence of a building equals the absence of God. We can end up building kingdoms on street corners rather than the kingdom of God on earth as it is in heaven.

I have to be honest here. I lead a church that owns buildings and has built buildings. But in the end, my heart, my passion is that we stop making the church *about* buildings. When we built our worship house at The Grove I asked our architect to keep the roofline below the tops of the trees, because from the street I hoped people would first see the grove of trees God grew instead of making a building the most prominent aspect of our church.

The church Jesus started was far more organic than the institution we have made it out to be. I don't see a New Testament pattern for the kind of church I've experienced most of my life, the kind dominated by bureaucracy, the kind with layers of committees, voting and ballots, members and nonmembers, constitutions and church governments. Instead, the early church was led by

Godly people who depended on guidance from the Spirit of God.

Systems Thinking

The scene from *Babies* says it all. In the 2010 documentary film following four individuals from birth to age one, a Japanese infant tries futilely to stack colored rings on a plastic pole. She's exasperated. She fusses and cries and falls backward in a fit, because she cannot get the colored rings to stack in proper order on the yellow pole.

From the day children are born in the developed world, we teach them to systemize. Our most rudimentary toys for infants, like this pole with colored doughnut rings, only works when everything is placed in correct order. Why? Why do we torture toddlers with symmetry?

Because we are convinced the world works better that way . . . and we think God likes it that way too.

With the seventeenth-century Age of Reason came the fundamental assumption that this world, this life, this existence could be reasoned out. The Bible and all its wealth of wonder about God and the way life is supposed to be was broken down into categories and matrices that explain His divine dealings with humanity. They dubbed it *systematic theology.*

The Enlightenment followed and began the process of

turning the Bible story into scientific text. Theologians became scientists.

One of the practices that came out of this was proof texting, which has turned the Bible narrative into a data bank. Proof texting is the practice of pulling unrelated scripture from random, unassociated passages to create apparent proof for an idea without adequate consideration for the context of the passages—such as when the "silencing passages" (in 1 Timothy 2 and 1 Corinthians 14) are used to keep women out of church leadership.

Here's what I'm *not* saying: it doesn't matter what you think. That's not true at all. I'm not saying to dumb down Christianity. I highly value education. I have a PhD from a divinity school; I get it. But somewhere along the way we've mistaken the means for the end. Orthodoxy is not the essence of our faith, nor is it how the kingdom of God is meant to be experienced.

But what we've done with all our systems is create a manageable God, one who fits neatly with Western analytics. And when we make the kingdom of God primarily a cognitive experience, it lets us sit easy with our dispassion and apathy toward broken places and hurting people. Because in our minds, we've got it right.

What if we're wrong?

How would we know? We look at Jesus. His teaching and what He valued—inclusion, embracing all people, lifting up the least, among others.

There are several character traits we must actively incorporate into our daily lives if we are going live authentic lives and have authentic faith.

Be Available

I was with Bob Goff for lunch and we shared a car ride back to his hotel after our meal. His cell phone must have rung a half a dozen times during the short trip. I told him he was nuts for putting his cell number in the back of his bestselling book about love. But that's just how Bob rolls.

"How many times a day does that ring?"

"Oh, maybe seventy or eighty times a day . . . but I don't answer if I'm eating with my wife, sweet Maria, and they can't leave a message." Like that helps the madness.

He answered every call that day, and with sincere enthusiasm. "Hey, Alice!" Or, "Tom, so great to hear from you. I'm with a friend right now, but I would love to talk more. Can you call back in about an hour?"

"So do you know Tom? Sounds like a friend," I wondered out loud.

"Nope, never talked to him in my life."

He spoke to every single person with genuine interest and complete focus. I loved it.

I think that's a lot like how Jesus lived each day.

Christ was always available, ready for the interruption. A

bleeding woman grabs His coat, so He stops to heal her. He's in the middle of delivering a message on a hillside amphitheater to an audience of five thousand when His disciples interrupt Him to say, "The people want lunch!" So He stops the preaching and starts feeding them. On another day He's preaching to a packed house—literally—when four guys interrupt His message by tearing a hole in the roof and lowering their wounded friend to His feet. Jesus drops His notes and picks him up.

Interruptions are opportunities, opportunities to be like Christ to people needing your attention, opportunities to serve and love.

Be Yourself

Jesus never tried to be anyone but Jesus, the son of a carpenter, the Son of God.

However, from the moment Jesus performed His first miracle, people wanted Him to be someone He was not. They wanted Him to be an anti-Caesar revolutionary. They wanted Him to be the king of the Jews. They wanted Him to be a pious traditionalist. But Jesus only wanted to be Jesus.

Jesus was chronically agitated by the inauthentic; He labeled them hypocrites. He said about the religious fakes, you polish up on the outside but rot on the inside. You parade around in your fancy clothes. It's a show, He said.

In my first year of being a lead pastor, I had a church member call to say, "Palmer, I heard you had your sons out past midnight last night and let them go to school late this morning. Is that true? And I heard it was a PG movie, and two of your sons are not thirteen."

Huh?

"Yeah, that's true," I answered. "And . . . ?"

"Well, I think people will judge you for that."

People or you? I wondered.

This is what had happened. It was opening night of *Star Wars: Episode III—Revenge of the Sith*, so I stood in line with my four sons (in elementary and junior high school) for two hours to catch the midnight showing.

We finally crawled into bed sometime after 3:00 a.m. It was one of our most memorable father-son nights. And I wasn't going to apologize for it.

So I calmly answered, "Yes, we had a great father-son night last night, and if your 'friends' want to judge me for that, let them judge me."

My encouragement to you is, be who you are. Be the best you, for your sons and daughters, for your wife or husband. Don't allow people to badger you into being someone you don't want to be.

I was with a well-known speaker waiting in the green room when the event organizer asked if he could bring in ten people who had won a contest to get a selfie with the speaker.

"Ah, I would rather not," he said. "I'm a bit of an intro-vert, and I think I would be slightly rattled when I get up to speak in a few minutes."

I loved his transparency. He just needed to be himself. He wasn't going to be pressured into putting on a gregarious act. Because that's not how God wired him, and that's okay. In fact, that is how we should live.

So often we try to be someone else.

The first time I met Bob a few years ago and heard him speak, I thought, *Wow, I need to speak like that. I need to be more animated. I need to buy a giant, floating, motorized bass to fly around the room like Bob. People would like me more if I delivered like Bob.*

But that's pure nonsense. Bob is Bob, and I just need to be Palmer. The best Palmer God made. Trying to be some-body you are not is exhausting and futile.

There is the best *you*. Just be that person.

Be Honest

Our church was brand-new, meeting in a junior high school gym soon to move onto our new campus, when Gordon called. "Palmer, I have an organ I want to donate to the church."

Wow. I was caught completely off guard. I never had plans for an organ. In fact, I did not want an organ for our new church. I wanted a band that would make people bring earplugs.

"Uh, okay, Gordon, that's awesome, but we cannot accept your kind gift . . ." I stammered, "because we have nowhere to store your organ during construction."

"Well, that is not a problem, Palmer. You can leave it in my garage until the building is done."

What was I supposed to say now? And this was a tough one. Gordon was a leader in our church, and he had been successful in business, and my guess was he tithed generously. If I said no, I could make him angry.

I decided to just be honest.

"Okay, I have to be straight with you, Gordon. We have no plans to ever have an organ in our new church. The high schoolers and college students simply are not composing music on organs anymore, Gordon, and the radio stations they listen to do not play organ music. So, sorry, but we cannot accept your free organ."

I could tell Gordon was disappointed by my answer, but I believe my honesty helped. Because he never brought up the organ thing again, and he was gracious enough not to hold it against me.

The problem is we tend to be pleasers. Christians are supposed to be that way—or so we think. Yes, be gracious and loving, but don't stop being authentic.

Because if we keep trying to please people, we can never be completely genuine.

Of course, hear people out on their creative ideas. But have the spine to say no when it's the right thing to say.

Be Vulnerable

I was bothered that a TV preacher had said God was judging Haiti because of sin and voodoo, and that's why Port-au-Prince fell in the earthquake of 2010.

So in a Sunday message when I talked about the true grace of God, I said, "If Port-au-Prince fell because of sin, why is Las Vegas still standing? Why am I still standing?"

I went on to explain that I—a pastor—am not perfect. I'm just not. I'm like every other parent doing my best to raise godly teenage sons. I've sometimes felt like a failure.

I told them all about feeling like a failure as a parent when the police woke me up because our sixteen-year-old broke curfew and was tooling around town with four buddies at three in the morning. Or when I had to stand in front of a judge with my eighteen-year-old who had jumped the wall of a stranger's home to go swimming with friends . . . at midnight—he said they were hot from playing basketball.

That's all I said. I didn't think I was saying anything profound, but that week I had person after person thank me for being transparent.

Vulnerability is dangerous—especially for those in ministry. (You get too transparent, and you get unemployed.)

There are boundaries, certainly. But we—all of us—should risk vulnerability sometimes. Why? Because even Jesus was honest enough to say to His Father, "Please take this cup of suffering away from Me."[3]

Pay Attention

Attention is one of the most powerful forces on earth.

We value the attention of people we look up to; maybe that's why we use economic language and say *pay* attention.

I realized I had a habit of looking past people who were talking to me when a very sweet woman at church put both hands on my face and said, "Please look me in the eye. I need to tell you something important."

I stopped looking over people's shoulders and started paying more attention to the person right in front of me.

My friend Josh is a well-known musician. After he plays or leads worship, he has this great way of sitting on the edge of the stage and talking to people as long as they wish. He never tries to end the conversation. He doesn't act like he's in a hurry or needs to be somewhere else.

Slow down. Give your attention away. It's precious to people near you; it's invaluable to the world we're called to be present to. Paying attention like Jesus did is taking notice of a person, regarding them as interesting or important regardless of their status or position.

When you look a person in the eye and focus, you say to them, "At this moment, you are the most important person in the universe."

And that's how it should be, because that's how you are to God.

Chapter 12

OUT OF BOXES OF SHAME

Box of Shame. Those were the words scrawled on the cardboard box in the lobby of the orphans' home in the opening scene of *Despicable Me*. A pair of eyes peeked hopefully through the small, crudely cut opening. They wanted out.

It makes me think about church. Those are the eyes of every Christian whose failures have been made public. We end up in the box of shame when people find out about our divorce, foreclosure, lost job, rebelling teen, addiction, unfaithful spouse, rejected college application, or debilitating sickness.

We all feel despicable, so we hide our scars. It's easier that way.

Shame keeps us from being honest about our struggles

and sorrow. I think it's because rebelling daughters, dirty addictions, and cheating spouses don't fit well with polished pews, red velvet carpet, and cheery preachers who gladhand you on your way out the door.

Some spend a lifetime hiding their shame. We all do, if we're honest. We want people around us to believe we are happier than we really are, more successful, and have less trouble.

That's why we hide our scars. I know that, because I have . . . literally.

When I first heard the word *precancerous*, my mouth went dry. My legs turned numb.

This was my first visit ever to a dermatologist, and when she said she had found basal-cell carcinoma, I stammered, "Well, cut it out! And make sure you get the whole thing!" It was the size of a Tylenol, but I wanted to be certain it was gone for good. (Many months later, my *new* dermatologist would explain that basal-cell carcinoma is relatively harmless.)

Unfortunately, this dermatologist had to move on to her next examination, so she sent in her intern, still in the very early stages of interning, I soon realized. She pulled out a scalpel and began to saw like she was cutting into a sirloin. Blood splattered everywhere. Panicked, she hollered for help, "I've got a bleeder!"

She finally sewed me up, with the touch of a ringside cut man.

When I finally pulled the bandages off at home and looked in the mirror, I gasped in horror. She had left me with a massive six-inch incision, just under my T-shirt line, in the middle of my chest! Large black sutures protruded from the hideous wound, making it look like a badly laced football. My first thought was, *Geez, I'll never again be able to wear deep V-neck T-shirts like Simon Cowell!*

A few weeks later, I was leaving for Cancún to perform a friend's wedding. Still bothered by the unsightly scar, I stopped by the mall and bought an imitation-gold medallion to hang over the massive incision. I wore the thing the entire week in Cancún.

I looked ridiculous, like Mr. T on the beach.

In hindsight, when I wonder why I tried so hard to hide my scar, I know it was because of shame. I didn't want my friends to think there was something wrong with Palmer.

Deep on the inside, all of us believe people will like us less and judge us more if they see our scars.

So we live with cheap medallions hanging over our wounds.

Cultures of Shame

Shame is worse than guilt.

Shame says, "What you did is who you are."

Guilt says, "I did something bad."

Shame says, "I am a bad person."

Guilt says, "I don't like what I did."

Shame says, "I don't like who I am: terrible, worthless, a failure."

The unfortunate truth is that in many churches and Christian organizations we seem to operate on a currency of shame. In fact, leaders have created cultures of shame.

Sometimes Christian leaders make shame worse by saying things like, "Your sin is why you suffer." Like the preacher on TV I mentioned who said, "God is judging Haiti for its voodoo." What kind of nonsense theology is that?

I was trying to fill up on bruschetta at a wedding reception in St. Louis, hoping the bride and groom would wrap up their postwedding photos and the call for dinner would come soon, when a young woman from California walked up and said, "You're a pastor, right?"

"Yes, I am," I mumbled, trying to take another unsatisfying bite of miniature toast and chopped tomato.

"Tell me this. Is it right what my friend's church just did to her? Her husband cheated on her. She left him. Her pastor told her to get back together with him. When she refused, the pastor put a picture of her on the big screen at church and announced that she was 'out of fellowship' because of sin in her life!"

"That's pretty messed-up."

"Yes, it is. So is that biblical?" She pressed.

"No, it's not. I've never heard of any church doing anything like that."

"Well, they do. And they did it to my friend."

Unbelievable.

The truth is, practically anyone who has walked through the doors of a church has been made to feel inadequate, judged, unworthy, unspiritual. In the modern church, Christians have exhausted each other with guilt and shame.

As a result, good people burn out and give up on church . . . or worse, they give up on God.

The fear of being judged by friends, parents, pastors, and God is one of life's deepest fears. It creates a kind of chronic depression. Deep down we believe our best is not good enough. So we just hope to cover it up and keep our mugs off the big screen.

I know parents who withhold love from their grown children to prove a point, to make them conform and perform.

God is not like that. God never withholds His love to make us act a certain way. When someone withholds love until we perform, or until we get it right, then love has been ruined. Love without expectations—free of conditions—is the driving theme of the Bible.

Jesus came to free us of our own exhausting attempts to deal with our shortcomings.

He made peace with everything in heaven and on earth by means of Christ's blood on the cross. This includes you who were once far away from God . . . He has brought you into His own presence, and you are holy and blameless as you stand before Him without blemish.

It's time for us to live in God's grace as Jesus embodied it.

The young woman at the wedding mentioned that the name of the church was Grace. Ironic, isn't it?

Christians love to talk about grace. We name our churches Grace, but grace like God's is in desperately short supply. His kind of grace is unnerving and, for the most part, unprecedented in the Christianity most of us know.

The truth is, God no longer sees you as the failed one or the messed-up one. Because the kind of grace Jesus talked about is one in which God only sees you as the precious one, the priceless one.

Grace is ultimately about a person being transformed from one who performs to one who loves. When we see a person transformed from addictive, angry, and vindictive to loving, we see the kingdom of God expand.

My hipster friend Ben serves on a church staff in So Cal. His church is not named Grace, but is definitely an icon of Jesus' kind of grace. The church sits smack in the middle of one of America's most affluent communities, but it is best known for attracting addicts and junkies, users and abusers—sinners. A lot like the crowd Jesus attracted. The last time I saw Ben, he talked about two young guys who had started attending their church. Both had been black-tar heroin addicts. The stuff is potent. It rotted out all their teeth.

Both young men gave their lives to Christ and showed up every Sunday with ear-to-ear toothless grins. It wasn't long, Ben said, before an oral surgeon at their church noticed. He invited them to his office and gave each recovered addict a bright new set of pearly whites.

Ben says the transformation was incredible . . . inside and out. He says on Sunday they won't stop smiling, wanting everyone to see their perfect new teeth and all.

I think that's how Jesus meant for grace in the church to work. Not for us to put each other in boxes of shame. Remember, God did not form you—the one and only unique, beautiful you—in order for you to hide. You are His stunning creation, "fearfully and wonderfully made," the Bible says. You are the one loved by God.

Jesus came to take away your shame. It hung on the cross with Him. All of your mistakes, all that's wrong about you, is left at the cross. When Christ enters the world of your life, all the shame dissolves, and you become the prized one—the deeply loved one.

You don't have to stay in the box of shame anymore.

One Easter, Pope Francis visited a detention center in Rome that housed young women sixteen to twenty-one years old. The young prisoners were asked to sit and wait. They lined the wall, beautiful, young women of every race, nationality, and religion, it seemed. When the pope arrived, he knelt in front of each of them and, one by one, untied their shoes, unbuckled their sandals, and washed their feet . . . then kissed them.[1]

The shamed and despised ones became the prized ones. It's like that for you.

Remember the stereotype of the Christians who have to impress each other and can't be vulnerable? Thank God, that image is fading—slowly. Today's Christians are learning to stop trying to act like they have it all together—acting like they don't sin. We should all be honest about our humanness—because of all the things that irritated Jesus it was the dishonesty and inauthenticity that seemed to bother Him the most. And dishonesty is always at odds with justice and stunts spiritual growth.

Part 3

Collective Faith:
The Passion for Justice

The age of reason is being eclipsed by the age of empathy."[1] That is how social theorist Jeremy Rifkin famously says it.

Rifkin is right. The church today swells with a new passion for justice, a passion that stretches beyond national boundaries and vast oceans. Our focal point lies beyond the boundaries of our own subcultures or church traditions. The walls our predecessors constructed between races and class and nations are tumbling down bit by bit.

Most important, we are starting to see the moral arc of the universe—and it bends toward justice. After years in the pastorate, I believe I see a critical factor that moves people beyond the shallow spiritual halfway mark and toward a faith and life that thrives—*justice*.

But today, a passion for justice is what is missing most in the personal lives of Christ followers and in the institution of the church. It's that key link to growing spiritually and deepening your relationship with God.

The Christian community stands divided on issues of spirituality and justice. Large camps of evangelicals have remained firm in their stance that our gospel is not about social justice. On the other side of the issue stand the millennials and tattooed hipsters who reject a gospel without justice and demand options for the poor, a response to oppression, and a spirituality that embraces mercy.

Jesus had a moment with a young, successful Jew who challenged Him by asking, "What must I do to inherit eternal life?"

After the young professional explained he had done everything required by the Torah, Jesus bluntly explained, "There's only one thing left to do: Sell everything you own and give it away to the poor."[2]

So the man says he started in Awana, went to camp, was baptized, joined a small group, did communion, tithed, even showed up for Wednesday night prayer and the Sunday evening vespers service, and Jesus says, "That's awesome, you're about halfway there. Now give your life away to serving and loving the least and the last."

That was the hard part. The man could not do it. But this is exactly what his spirituality needs to grow and thrive.

Jesus' point in the entire exchange is, you can do all the

right religious things, but if you do not pursue justice and love with compassion, then you fall short of the kingdom of God.

How are you doing at letting people who feel marginalized know they matter? Or, what are you doing to stop the sale of young girls for sex in far away places in Asia or close to home in Atlanta? Or, in what way are you working to curb the spread of Ebola in West Africa? What have you done recently to help immigrant poor in your community know you are glad they are your neighbors?

Because if you are doing none of these things—or anything else to balance the scales of justice in the world—then I know there is a facet of your spirituality going dormant, atrophying on the inside, keeping you from fully becoming the person God made you to be.

But don't be disheartened, there is a way to change that.

Collective Faith

Collective faith is the sixth and most striking, yet elusive, stage of spiritual development. It's the highest stage. This kind of faith is marked by the grace of an others-focused life. Stage-six people are highly concerned with justice and compassion, more than self-preservation and egocentrism. They realize their most biblical calling is to give themselves away to make this world whole, to heal lives, to show others the sweetness of knowing God.

James Fowler explains the spirit of universalizing faith like this:

> Persons described by stage six typically exhibit qualities that shake our usual criteria of normalcy. Their heedlessness to self-preservation and the vividness of their taste and feel for transcendent moral and religious actuality give their actions and words an extraordinary and often unpredictable quality. In their devotion to universalizing compassion they may offend our parochial perceptions of justice. In their penetration through the obsession with survival, security, and significance they threaten our measured standards of righteousness and goodness.[3]

A primary indication that a person is reaching stage six is their willingness to sacrifice their own well-being for the good of others. Fowler explains this kind of sacrifice with the word *subversive*. This person's position and mission are radically different from the rest of culture. They give their complete focus, attention, and life to change the circumstances of the marginalized, abused, and exploited. They are willing to risk their own safety to help the helpless. "Heedless of the threats to self . . . Stage 6 becomes a disciplined, activist *incarnation*—a making real and tangible—of the imperatives of absolute love and justice."[4]

People at stage six abandon the natural human tendency to gravitate toward self-preservation and live engrossed with one's own life and well-being. A steady broadening in social awareness eclipses the egocentrism of the less mature years.[5] When people begin to live this way, they shatter the limited perceptions of justice that have created rampant dispassion in so many Christian circles. They threaten the old standards of righteousness and goodness and create a new morality, rooted more in bringing shalom to earth than in personal piety.

Others-Focused Lives

Dallas Willard made the most revealing observation when he said that egocentrism is the primary indicator of shallow spirituality.

Conversely, the others-focused life leads toward the deepest kind of spirituality.

This is what Jesus so often taught.

He shared the famous illustration of two ways to live— either crossing the street to avoid the other or walking purposefully toward the other.

Jesus reminds us the road of life is littered with hurting people who need love. A friend loses her job. A son fails a test. An immigrant needs work. A coworker cannot pay their bills. A village drinks filthy water. A husband is ridiculed by his wife. A high school senior is left at home on prom night.

So I ask, who has God put in your life for you to care for? Because Jesus put you in the life-saving business.

In Jesus' story, the religious ones walked on by to the other side of the road. They moved far away from the desperate one.

Then a different kind of person came along. His skin tone was different, He dressed differently, His language was different, and He lived differently than the seemingly religious ones. The different one then did the most astonishing thing: He moved toward the other. He showed compassion and demanded justice. This is the kind of spirituality most desired by God.

With this in mind, the church today must focus its attention on engaging its culture for Christ and changing the world for good. It's time for you to give your life to God's kingdom mission on earth. Not somebody else. You.

Leonard Sweet's blunt honesty on the subject of compassion is incredibly refreshing:

The compassion furnace burned brightly in Christianity's natal days. Souls forged and fired in the ovens of service went on to warm others with good deeds and good news. That's how the church exploded. Now our compassion furnace is going dark. . . .

Too much postmodern spirituality equates sacred space with only that which lies between both ears. Sacred space in a biblical spirituality bring together the internal space of joy, peace, contentment, and meaning with the external space of justice, harmony, truth, and compassion.[6]

The kind of following that pleases God is when you "share your food with the hungry and to provide the poor wanderer with shelter—when you see the naked, to clothe them, and not to turn away from your own flesh and blood? Then your light will break forth like the dawn."[7]

The prophet Amos says the same thing, but his words sting:

I hate, I despise your religious festivals; your assemblies are a stench to me. . . . Away with the noise of your songs! I will not listen to the music of your harps. But let justice roll on like a river.[8]

Ouch.

So God is fed up with our religious shows and performance, and instead wants us to be more about showing compassion and doing justice?

How are we doing at that?

Christians for the past hundred years have been good at creating a gospel that changes the way we think, or changes the way we behave in our personal lives, in a private kind of way—not necessarily changing the way we act toward others.

But I believe most of us want to bring right offerings to God—the offering of our best selves. How do we do it? We can start by getting good at recognizing injustice when we see it—and figuring out how to turn it around.

Chapter 13

JESUS JUSTICE

Not long after I left Malawi, Nelson Mandela arrived for an official visit. As Malawian president Bakili Muluzi and Mandela made the slow drive through the capital city, Mandela waved for the limousine to stop when he noticed the curb was lined with the crippled. They are the ones who grip blocks of wood in their fists to shuffle themselves along the sidewalks of Lilongwe, begging for food.

As he often did, Mandela climbed out of the limousine and, one by one, took time to meet the disabled of Lilongwe. The line on the curb was long, all the people sitting on the filthy edge of the coarse concrete sidewalk. Finally, obviously frustrated, Mandela turned to President Muluzi and, in front of a crowd of media, demanded, "Why are all of these crippled people sitting on the dirty street and not in wheelchairs?"

Clearly embarrassed, Muluzi mumbled a shamed, "I don't know."

Never one to mince words, Mandela announced, "You need to know! Mr. President, the crippled and the poor of Malawi are your responsibility."[1]

Jesus said the same kind of thing about you and me and our role as keepers of this world for God, that the poor and afflicted are our responsibility—not somebody else's.

Social justice is when you lift the man up off the curb and sit him in a wheelchair, restoring his dignity.

We need to start our justice conversation by looking at Jesus Himself. One of the great reasons God sent His Son from heaven to earth was to give us a model of how to live toward others—especially the least and the last.

Jesus showed us a way to live that gave dignity to foreigners and women, He stopped to care for the sick, He shared meals with the social outcasts, He comforted people in sorrow, He spoke out against oppression, He pulled children up from the bottom rung of society and put then on top and said heaven was for them. And then He gave this soul-piercing speech at the end of His life, saying, if you do not follow my example and live this way, then you can never be a part of my kind of kingdom.[2]

❦

Justice is the pursuit of balance.

Social justice is about helping society regain its moral equilibrium. It means confronting oppression when you see it. It means at your very core being fundamentally bothered by—and against—oppression of any kind.

Social justice is the pursuit of equal advantages for all people in a community, the intentional distribution of good within a society. It involves the collective and personal commitment to help others and treat all people equally, removing inequality—without prejudice—regardless of nationality, race, gender, wealth, religion, or any other factor.

Justice is not charity. Christians have been good at charity. Justice is different. Justice provides the grounding for charity. Justice gets at the root of why a person needs charity.

For example, handing the crippled Malawian on the street curb fifty kwachas is charity. Remaking a system that provides wheelchairs to the lame and meaningful employment for the handicapped is justice.

Justice is caring for the poor and helping them dig out of their poverty trap. A God-centered theology of society is structured to give advantage to certain segments of our population that need more help—and that's okay—righting systemic injustice. When we live this way, we allow the poor to experience God as embodied by Jesus.

We must be willing to honestly admit that those in the first world, the West, have benefited for centuries from an unjust, out-of-balance system.

We do not pursue justice out of guilt, trying to make up for the greed or bigotry of past generations; nor is this a demonizing of the privileged. But this is about becoming aware of our privileged status and being intentional about providing preferential options for the poor.

The good news is the next-generation church has ignited the justice fire already. Unfortunately, many are not sure what to do about their burning. Some feel guilty, inadequate, or confused and end up doing nothing. My challenge to you is to grab on to the issue of structural injustice that God has weighed on your soul and begin to balance the scales.

What is your responsibility in creating a more just society?

Seeing and acknowledging is the first step. The next is to speak up—because to ignore injustice is to condone it.

Here are a few examples of injustices we all at times have ignored.

Injustice Is When a Person Faces Bias Because of His or Her Race

A former student in my ministry, Lincoln, said he couldn't take it anymore. Practically every week the local police turned on their lights, asked to see his ID—and most troubling—asked what he was doing in Wheaton, a sleepy bedroom community west of Chicago.

Wheaton was Mayberry. Lincoln was from Trinidad and Tobago. He was built like a linebacker, sported a fauxhawk, and wore tank tops all summer. The truth is, Lincoln looked fairly intimidating.

Lincoln would explain to the police that he was a grad student and had every right to be in Wheaton. But the lights kept flashing in his rearview mirror. His crime? The color of his skin.

Finally, after about four weeks in a row of being pulled over, Lincoln drove down to the police station and asked to see the chief—walking in with his fauxhawk and muscles bulging out of his tank top. Surprisingly, the chief sat down with him and listened as Lincoln shared about the harassment in his city. Then Lincoln told the chief he wanted to hold a diversity seminar for his officers. Lincoln is pretty assertive that way. The chief agreed, and the next week all the officers who had stopped him over the past few months had to listen as Lincoln shared what it is like for a black man to drive through an affluent, white suburban community.

When a black man can drive through any community anywhere without fear of wanton harassment, then the scales of justice finally begin to balance.

I know a little about racial bias personally, because that is how I felt when the Liberian kids called me a scraped hog, a pejorative term for white people.

Today, my friends laugh when I tell them the story and so can I, but when I was ten, the words burned like coals on my skin.

Growing up in Liberia, if I fouled a kid too hard on the soccer field or got into a vehement argument over the score of a Ping-Pong game, the mean kids always called me the same thing: "scraped hog!"

When Liberians cook a hog they place the entire pig, skin and all, over the open fire. The meat cooks slowly on the inside, but on the outside the skin chars and burns. When the pig is removed from the fire, they take a knife and scrape away all the burned flesh, leaving in its place a sickly, pinkish-white scraped hog.

And that's what they called me because of the color of my skin.

When I hear people today make derogatory comments about a person's character, or stereotype them based on the color of their skin, I cringe. It feels wrong to the core that we judge people or treat them a certain way because of skin color.

Over the last hundred years, no voice for justice—

particularly in the conversation on racism—has equaled that of Martin Luther King, Jr., who famously declared, "Injustice anywhere is a threat to justice everywhere."[3]

Injustice Is When a Girl in Pakistan Is Shot in the Head Because She Wants to Attend School

Malala Yousafzai grew up in the remote Pakistan Swat Valley, a Taliban-controlled region. As the Taliban's influence grew, so did their demand that girls not attend school. The Taliban has no issue with boys being in school; it is the girls they don't allow.

Do you see how the scales of justice fall out of balance? At just eleven years old, daring Malala gave a fiery speech in the region's capital of Peshawar. She titled her talk "How Dare the Taliban Take Away My Basic Right to Education?"

This kind of brutal honesty did not sit well with the Taliban. Just weeks later, on her way home from school, a gunman boarded her bus and shot Malala in the head . . . for attending school.

Bullets were not enough to silence this voice for justice. Malala has since healed, and her voice is even louder, insisting that girls everywhere have a right to education. And now her bravery has been recognized with the Nobel Peace Prize.

Because that is what is fair and just.

Injustice Is When You Are Forced to Cover Your Face Because of Your Gender

It is time to stop hiding the faces of daughters and sisters and wives and mothers in the name of religion. Set them free. The burka is a shaming shackle.

The first time I walked past a woman in a full-faced black burka, I stopped dead in my tracks. It was not in the outback of some dusty, remote Afghan village. We were shopping in a mall in Johannesburg. It could have been a polished mall in Orange County.

I turned around to catch up with the couple, a man followed by his wife in the black burka covering her face, when my wife grabbed my arm. With all the strength she could muster, she held on, asking through clenched teeth, "What are you doing?"

She knew my tendency to be impulsive.

"I just want to tell her she doesn't have to wear that mask anymore. That's all," I said innocently.

She wouldn't let go of my arm.

Today I still want to say to all women forced to hide behind the burka, "You do not have to wear the dark veil anymore. You are beautiful and treasured by God and the rest of us. And no man has the right to demand that you cover your face, perfectly shaped in the *imago dei.*"

It's time for all of us to help end this senseless oppression. It's not truly a religious issue; the Koran has no such requirement that women cover their faces.

Egyptian journalist and writer Mona Eltahawy paints a haunting picture of what it's like to live under the shroud of the suffocating burka. Educated woman loathe it. The male-dominated societies of the Middle East guilt, shame, and beat women into wearing the hideous burka. "The men say pearls are hidden, that's why we cover you up, because we prize you," she writes.[4] But that's a lie. It's the insecurity and jealousy of the men who keep their wives' faces hidden in public.

This problem is also not a cultural issue. I have undergraduate and graduate degrees in cultural anthropology (intercultural studies), so I do not say these things glibly or carelessly. Simply because a practice is considered "cultural," or is culturally accepted, does not make it right. Some cultural practices are absolutely wrong, like forcing a woman to hide her face.

Injustice Is When Powerful People Steal Your Land and Banish You to a Wasteland

I was in Washington State having a salmon cookout on the beach. My family met at the farthest northwest tip of the United States, Cape Flattery. It is a windswept, rocky, remote corner of the country—and a Native American Indian reservation. The weathering town of Neah Bay sits nearby, the center of the local Makah community. As I drove past some of the dilapidated homes, I thought, *Is this the best we can do?*

When we take a people's land and exile them to a barren desert or a remote northwestern wilderness, that is injustice.

Some injustices will take centuries to right.

Injustice Is When Fathers Sell Their Daughters for Sex

My heart broke on a recent trip to Thailand. I knew I had to do something, I started by writing a letter to the Thai ambassador of the United States. I'm still waiting for his reply. Here is what I wrote:

> An Open Letter to All the Fathers of Daughters in Thailand:
> Just hours ago I landed on American soil. My heart still aches from what I saw on the streets of your towns and cities— your daughters for sale.
> I write to say, Stop selling your daughters.
> I am told you are selling your daughters because it keeps the hotel rooms booked, the restaurants filled, and the tourists' baht flowing.
> But I say you don't have to sell your daughters.
> I've traveled the globe—from Costa Rica to Cuba to Ivory Coast—and the beauty of your mountains and beaches and people are unequaled. Sell your beauty, not your daughters.
> I traveled high in the Thanon Thong Chai Range to sample

coffee grown by the Karen people. The rich aroma of shade-grown coffee hung thick in the air. When we sampled the hand-sorted pea-berry coffee, the flavor lingered for hours. I am an aspiring coffee aficionado, and yours was some of the best I've tasted. Sell your coffee and stop selling your daughters.

Bangkok was a culinary adventure. We sampled gang keow wan and pad thai in the restaurants. Had chiang mai noodles on the street at night. We tried skewers of beef and chicken barbecued over open-charcoal fires in halved fifty-gallon drums. Ate green curry, red curry . . . and hot chilies until our eyes watered. Everything was extraordinarily delicious. So sell your cuisine, not your daughters.

Your beaches in Pattaya were breathtaking. We swam the balmy waters of the Gulf of Thailand. The palm-lined beaches stretched as far as the eye could see until they vanished beyond the peninsula cliffs. But just steps from the sand, the streets were crowded with the worst the world has to offer: pedophiles and sex tourists. Their leering presence robbed the beauty. The strange absence of laughing children vacationing by the sea was deafening. Nor did we see striking young couples on honeymoons or weekend getaways. All you have attracted to your stunning beaches are the aged deviants staring at and groping your daughters for sale. Don't you know that if you stop selling your daughters, your beaches and seaside hotels will burst with excited families and couples in love? So sell your beaches and stop selling your daughters.

Maybe you don't know, but in the eyes of the world your entire country has become a seedy Las Vegas strip club, or the red-light district of Amsterdam. You are listed right there with them, because we are onto you. Your karaoke bars are not for singing, your massage parlors are not for aching backs, and your nightclubs are not for dancing. The charade is over. You fool no one. Your reputation has slithered to the gutter.

All because you believe selling your daughters makes your economy thrive. It's not worth it. It's time for you to stand up as fathers and mothers and men and women who lead your country and end this lasciviousness. Your daughters are far more precious than the rubles or rupees, pesos or pounds, euros or dollars. Your cowardly attempt to build an economy on the backs of your daughters is not working.

I don't say any of this to hurt you, Thailand. I say this because after just a seven-day visit, I love your country. I've been struck by its beauty and the warm kindness of your people. But my heart aches for your daughters.

I write to warn you that good people around the world who care about your daughters will stop traveling to your places of beauty and intrigue.

So I challenge you to enforce your laws, to prosecute the pimps and mamasans who sell your girls. Stand up to the Russian mafia that runs your hotels. You don't need their dirty business. Kick the bums out. Instead, invite the ecotourists, the cultural tourists, and the adventure tourists—and stop pandering to the sex tourists. They ruin your good name.

Stop selling your daughters, because when you do, you turn your country into the world's brothel . . . and yourself into the pimp.

There are so many more examples of injustice. It wears countless faces: hate crimes, child labor, human trafficking, gender discrimination, the cost of higher education, inaccessible health care, commercial farming that puts local growers out of business, monopolies, and the role of women in the church. I list only a few. Injustice remains widespread and rampant today—and Jesus still wants justice.

Chapter 14

JUSTICE CONVERSION

One of our great God-given purposes on earth is to right the scales of justice for all.

It's time to balance the scales.

What is needed in the church today is the call to a conversion that runs deeper than the mind, a conversion that radically alters the moral bearing of the soul. A conversion toward justice.

In the previous chapter I shared examples of injustice. Now I'm offering a way forward, a way to change personally, a way to change everything—a justice conversion.

Justice as the Transforming Experience

What causes people to change? In what ways do they change? These are the spiritual formation questions that Christian educators and theologians have been asking for centuries.

Spiritual formation is primarily a transformation of the soul—a combination of a changed mind, emotions, and volition. In short, it's a discovery of a new way of being. A new way of living in this world that far surpasses something we only know in our minds or believe in our hearts.

Over my years in ministry I have repeatedly watched the transforming experience Christ followers undergo when they encounter oppression and injustice for the first time. I have vividly seen how God uses life's most disturbing experiences to shape the soul—in a way and to a degree that will never happen from the comfort of a suburban cul-de-sac.

Like the college student who leaned over to me on a plane ride back from Cuba to say, "This is the first time in my life I saw God step down from heaven to work in my life." Or the soccer mom who turned to me in the middle of an African village to say, "Now I know Jesus." Or the school principal who returned from Haiti and said, "I am a different person now." Or the twenty-year-old recovering alcoholic who said to me before boarding the plane, "I can never live the same again." She didn't. She can't. She's been transformed. All justice conversions.

Justice Disturbs the Soul

I want to introduce you to an idea and coin a phrase: *soul disequilibration*. Before your eyes glaze over, let me explain.

Educators widely agree that in order for a person to reach higher stages of understanding and cognitive development, they usually must first experience disequilibration—or cognitive dissonance—the disturbing of the mind with new or previously unaccepted information.

For example, when Galileo said the earth was not the center of the universe, he was put on trial for heresy. No one could fathom a spinning earth. Who would suggest such a thing? Audacious. The information was so new, going into such uncharted mental territory, it spawned anger and violence. To spare being burned at the stake, Galileo was forced to announce his ideas as being "abjured, cursed, and detested." And that's how it stayed, until 350 years later, when the Catholic Church finally admitted Galileo was right and it was wrong.[1] It took the Catholic Church centuries to admit its fault. Nobody relishes disequilibration.

In a previous work, I explained how walking into the homes of the broken disturbs us spiritually. Here I want to extrapolate on that idea to say there is an aspect, a kind of spiritual formation, that happens only when we go to the most blighted places to be among the most desperate people.

Simply put, in order for us to reach the highest stages of

spiritual maturity, we must first experience a disequilibration of the soul—*soul disequilibration.*

When you sit in the pew of an air-conditioned church or on the cozy couch of a living room in a small group, your soul can only be transformed to a degree: about halfway. Not until you leave the comfort of your sectional and the safe confines of your neighborhood church can God complete the transforming work on your soul. What the soul craves most and needs for ultimate change is to be disturbed, bothered, and broken . . . and then remade.

When you hold an orphaned Haitian toddler in your arms . . . it disturbs your soul.

When you bandage a festering tropical ulcer in the Sapo jungle . . . it disturbs your soul.

When you walk though tear gas choking the streets of a St. Louis suburb . . . it disturbs your soul.

When you sit by the bed of a man dying of AIDS . . . it disturbs your soul.

And then your spirituality grows. And expands.

And your soul is transformed in brand-new ways.

And you realize what a justice conversion of the soul is all about.

Sunan, a young Thai woman, walked into my office unannounced. She was bubbly and talked excitedly about the things she had heard at The Grove. Sunan said she was a new Christian and had traveled three hundred miles from her home in Corona, California, to see me and ask for my advice on what she should do with her life.

A pretty daunting question when I did not know Sunan at all. So I asked her to tell me about her passions and what bothered her in this world. I hit a nerve. Her eyes welled with tears as she told me about the girls for sale on the streets of Bangkok, her family's home before emigrating to America.

She went on. "I've been dreaming of starting a ministry that would help rescue the girls and put them through school, but when I shared my idea with a woman at my church, she said, 'Sunan, you are a new Christian. You can't start a ministry like that yet. You need to stay here at church and mature before you do something like that.'"

I just sat there for a few minutes without saying anything. I had to think about that one: how churches empower dispassion, downplay the need, and instead tell us to give more money and join a small group. Finally, I answered, "Sunan, first, I absolutely love your passion and completely resonate with your desire to rescue exploited girls. Here's my advice to you: begin your ministry now. I'm sorry to say, your church friend has it upside down and backward. We grow when we give our lives away. We grow when God is using our lives to change what is messed up in this world. We grow when we live for something and someone far greater than our personal well-being. Tell your friend she's wrong. There's no more waiting. Your time to start changing this world for Christ is now."

Carpe diem. Now is the time.

Sunan's church experience is a microcosmic example of what is wrong with the church today. We keep telling people that spiritual change happens inside the four walls of our redbrick buildings with the white steeples on top. We tell them that spiritual maturity transpires in the head, and a changed life means they stop watching so much *Real Housewives of Orange County*.

And when we do that, instead of growing into deeply spiritual and inspired Christ followers, we create pious, dispassionate people. And that's why many Christians never grow a deep, meaningful relationship with God. They settle for being half the person God intended. They end up stuck halfway.

What is needed today is a *justice conversion*.

We need a confession and conversion away from our spiteful attitudes toward immigrants and the poor and our racial stereotypes—toward a spirituality drenched with compassion and love for all.

To live justly is more than *not* being racist, or *not* taking advantage of the desperate. To live justly means we actively work to create a culture that is intrinsically just.

If this is going to become true in our personal lives, then we must begin to make real changes to how we live, how we treat people, how we spend money, what we do with our vacation time and our excess. It starts by being with the least and the last.

It means closing the distance you have allowed between you and the other.

It means doing justice.

Do Justice

The contemplative Brennan Manning writes my favorite description of the passion of the Christ: "Jesus spent a disproportionate amount of time with people described in the Gospels as the poor, the blind, the lame, the lepers, the hungry, sinners, prostitutes, tax collectors, the persecuted, the downtrodden . . . the rabble who know nothing of the law, the crowds, the little ones, the least, the last, and the lost sheep of Israel.

In short, Jesus hung out with ragamuffins."[2]

If this was Jesus' way of being in the world, then shouldn't we—His apprentices—*do* the same?

We see a pattern in the life of Jesus that He made *doing*

justice His everyday business: He included the excluded. He touched the lepers—literally. He challenged the inequality of women. He embraced the chased-away children.

Jesus defied the racism of His day. He refused to treat the Samaritans (the immigrants of first-century Israel) as second-class citizens.

He also rejected religious bigotry. He included the tax collectors, prostitutes, and town drunks. He became an advocate for the poor, the hungry, the sick, and the prisoner.

And He did all He could to balance the scales.

Pursuing justice like Jesus is what collective faith is all about, and it's a primary indicator of spiritual maturity.

That is what we see in Scripture.

The spiritually shallow do not understand justice.

Justice is a sign of depth, because it means a person has placed the needs of another in front of their own. They risk their own safety to help the poor and the powerless. We see this manifest in the most unexpected ways.

- A business owner willing to profit less in order to provide adequate health care for their employees.

- A doctor risking her own well-being to travel to Liberia to help end an Ebola outbreak.

- An employee risking his job to speak up on behalf of a coworker who is passed over for a promotion because of gender or race.

A Church Movement Toward Justice

This is the entire point of *Justice Calling*—in order to mature and reach the upper stages of faith and truly experience Christ, the people of God must pursue justice and do love. The good news is its not just individual Christians pursing justice. I see a new kind of church emerging, a church for justice. I see this new Church reembracing the Bible's call to social justice in several critical areas:

Sustainability

It used to be that Christians widely ignored sustainability efforts and inner-city problems. Not anymore.

Church-driven initiatives like Bonton Farms are remaking blighted neighborhoods. In the gritty south Dallas community of Bonton, no grocery store chain will open their doors. Two liquor stores sell overpriced milk and few food items. The round-trip bus ride to the nearest grocery store takes three hours. By USDA standards, Bonton is a *food desert*.

That is why Trog Trogdon left his church job in the suburbs to become an urban farmer in Bonton. He and a crowd of Bonton neighbors are taking abandoned inner-city plots and turning them into flourishing gardens of food.

Something very biblical, something Edenic, is happening in Bonton.

Women

Several years ago, the church I serve in Arizona licensed our first woman pastor. It was a proud day for all of us in leadership. I waited, however, for the backlash. For the emails and phone calls and angry conversations in the courtyard from the voices who object to women in ministry. The best news is that there was not one negative response. Then I invited her to preach. Her message was spectacular. But again I waited for opposition. It never came. I realized our church, like many churches, has entered a new day for women, giving them the respect, dignity, and equal value they deserve.

My only regret is that it took too long. In hindsight, I wish I had pushed sooner for equality in the pulpit. I regret giving women the title director when they were truthfully serving as pastors. When churches do this, they devalue women and even take from them financially, because females are robbed of the equal tax advantages awarded to male pastors. It struck me that doing this—and many church still do—is unethical. Dishonest. Unbiblical.

Abolition

In the kind of church I was raised in, no one said words like *prostitute* and *pimp*, or used phrases like *sex trafficking* and *sex worker*. It was all too crass and distant for talk among sophisticated Presbyterians.

The good news is a movement is swelling of Christians who are giving their lives to stopping the sexual exploitation of girls and women. END IT does not even refer to itself as an organization, but as a movement. Its mission, they say, is to shine a light on sex slavery and end the bondage of women everywhere. They call their volunteer abolitionists freedom fighters.

Movements like this are remaking the church into what Christ originally intended.

Social Entrepreneurs

A quiet revolution is turning the tide on global poverty. I see the church moving away from being a people who use charity as a way to appease guilt or to manipulate people into the church. Instead, a host of entrepreneurs who profit for good, for society—social entrepreneurs—are rising up to empower entire communities. They are seeking foundational change, trying to *do the most good possible.*

One of my favorite examples is 31 Bits, founded by five fashion-loving college students in Orange County, California. In their junior year they visited Uganda, and the trip was life altering. They met women who survived war and had nothing. Most shocking, they say, was that the young women were their age. Early twenties—scarred, scared, and starving for food, hungry for love. Some of the women they met were making stunning jewelry out of old posters. The

Vanguard University students realized all the women needed was a market. They thought, "We know fashion and we know a lot of fashion-loving people live in Orange County."

So 31 Bits (the name taken from Proverbs 31) was born, they say, to revolutionize the way consumers consume.[3] Their goal is to help us see that our purchasing can have either a positive impact or a negative one. Their mission is to lift up the artist and creator and connect them in a meaningful way with the customer. Artisans in their program receive a sustainable income, enough for them and their children to receive an education and dig out of their poverty pit.

The most mature followers of Jesus Christ will sacrifice for the cause of justice. It's collective faith, faith that is heedless to self-preservation. At this stage, you'll see the world dramatically differently than the rest of society. You will identify with the poor, the crushed, and the exploited, and give your best to right the scales of injustice—just like Jesus.

Chapter 15

OUTWARD-FOCUSED LIVES

Becky is thirty-eight years old and a devoted wife, has three kids, and lives in the burbs. Her kids' soccer balls roll around the minivan floor as she taxies them to school, cheer practice, and piano lessons. She loves her church and leads a small group on Wednesdays. But she is stressed from her hurried schedule, growing bills, and the committees she serves on at church.

And Becky always listens to Christian radio.

Becky is the bull's-eye of the Christian music industry's target audience. Every producer, composer, and musician knows her well. They know if their music does not make Becky happy, they will never get play on the Christian radio stations that cover the country.

My singer-songwriter friend David says Becky turns Christian radio vanilla, bland, and boring. "Becky" represents everything that's safe and traditional.

David says producers at his label say things like, "David, you can't write about boy soldiers in Africa with AKs and children sold for sex in Asia. You're stressing Becky out. She needs something safe for the whole family. Change your lyrics. Sing with less aggression. Tone down your beat. Write something positive and encouraging."

David quit the label. He says he's tired of being labeled for Becky.

Now he writes what he feels compelled by God to say. He writes about poverty and injustice and abuse and wanton violence. He's trying to stop it all.

Because he knows men and women like "Becky" never will.

Sadly, our church pews fill with these kinds of apathetic people. So our pastors write sermons for them, and our church programs target them.

In the end, we've manufactured a brand of Christianity that is safe, isolated, and dispassionate about the wrong in the world so complacent people can be comfortable.

Becoming Missional

Before entering the messy but exhilarating world of church-planting, my experience was that churches poured most of their resources and energy into making their own church run—they were consumed with feeding the church machine.

Today we need to turn the focus of the church outward.

The first value I championed at our new church-plant was to be missional.

Missional does not mean "missions." Stick with me here—I love missions. I even grew up an MK (missionary kid). But it is not simply a department of your church—and in many places, an afterthought at that. Missional is the entire purpose of the church, the heartbeat. Mission is your raison d'être. It's your prima facie duty. The most important thing you will ever give your life to.

Here's what I mean when I use the term *missional*.

In recent years, the word has grown in popularity and acceptance. In order not to miss out on the next hot trend, many churches and leaders have latched onto the word without really understanding what the movement is all about. Some feature it on their websites while they have no real missional impetus at all.

At the heart of the missional movement is the idea of the *missio Dei*—the mission of God. Pioneers in the missional movement Michael Frost and Alan Hirsch describe it like this: "The missional church is a sent church. It is a going church; a movement of God through his people; sent to bring healing to a broken world."[1]

Christ came to do so much more—in and through your life—than only to save you from hell after you die. God's purpose for you is to live *on mission*. He uses people like you and me to repair and heal the world we live in. For example, God's call to Abraham, and in turn Israel, was that "the whole world will be blessed through you."[2] Your life is meant to be a blessing to others . . . now. Today.

Missional living is when the church (that's you, Christians everywhere) gives itself away to serve the world. This is collective faith. What is good about God's kingdom is not just good for you and me; it is good for all people. "What Jesus was to the church, the church must now be for the world."

Inward-Focused People

The church of tomorrow must rediscover its *sentness*.

We tend to look in. We love to gaze in the mirror. We are an innately narcissistic people. But we have huddled behind the walls of our "sanctuaries" long enough. It's time to get out and live as Jesus called us to live.

It seems like the American Christian is under the impression that our goal is to get people to come to church, and once they are in, to teach them how to get more people to come to church. As though the entire purpose of the Christian life is to go to church. But when you do that, the church becomes about attending a meeting, not living the good news. That's why I say we are a people called to live *on mission* for God. You are called to go love, heal, free, protect, serve, encourage, and share . . . in the name of Jesus.

A close friend of mine who has taught in Africa for years was recently back at his home church. He was scheduled for a Sunday-morning interview at all three services. Before he was allowed to take the stage, the senior pastor and executive pastor sat him down to say, "We need you to know we have our own operational needs here. So you can't talk about any of the needs you are experiencing in Africa. We know our people will give generously if you ask them, but we need their money here."

I'm not making that up. That was it, verbatim. Generation Excess had moved into the suburban church.

We've heaped our plates full while every day millions go hungry. That's a problem.

And I'm not saying the really glib thing your grandmother used to say: "Clean your plate; there are starving babies in Africa." What I *am* saying is maybe we've piled too much on the plate to begin with. Maybe we've taken too large a portion. Maybe we live too much for ourselves and care too little about others.

I'll always remember the time I held out my plate for

Mary to fill it at a Serve the World dinner. She hardly gave me enough for a third-grader. "Hey, I eat more than that," I said with a laugh.

"Sorry," she answered gently. "I quit heaping plates with food when I came home from Malawi."

Without any prodding, she explained, "I was filling plates with food at COTN's feeding center when we ran out. It never crossed my mind that the food would run out. It was my fault. I had piled heaps of food on the kids' plates. I wanted them to eat well that night. But then the food ran out, and more than fifty children were still in line. They all went home hungry. I cried myself to sleep that night. That's why I've quit heaping food on plates."

And so should we.

My brother, Paul, is the president of African Bible Colleges, with campuses in Liberia, Malawi, and Uganda. He recently asked a good friend if he would talk to his pastor about allowing the college to present its scholarship program to their congregation. His friend was certain his pastor would resonate with the idea.

Wrong.

Highly embarrassed, his friend called back with his pastor's response. "He said he can't let you do that, Paul. He said he's afraid people would start giving too much to Africa and not enough to running our church." In other words, the pastor believed his people had enough for his kingdom in America but not enough for God's kingdom in Africa.

Maybe he's right. Most of that church's people live in a struggling California city you may have heard of: the Orange County "poverty center" of Newport Beach.

Try to believe the bad math God uses when He says, "Test Me in this and see if I don't open up heaven itself to you and pour out blessings beyond your wildest dreams."

Missional living happens when you reject apathy, when you move from dispassionate to empathetic, when you leave your kingdom of comfort and indifference and commit to spread God's kingdom of hope and love and grace and beauty.

Missional living is when you realize it's not just about you. That's the part that really bothers people. People want church "for me." I hear it all the time. But it's not about you, it's about the mission of God.

Many churches spend a majority of their time, energy, and resources trying to keep people already at church happy. I think that's why a church in Texas has a beauty salon. That's why a church in California has nine different worship service styles, including a rock-and-roll service (it comes with fog machines and a lot of distortion), café worship (outdoors with coffee), hula worship (worship with sounds from the islands), and, of course, country worship (my guess is that means line dancing and NASCAR updates).

If you think about it, much of what happens in churches is focused inward. The programs are for people already there. Only those on the inside understand the language, like *ministry, tithe, the koinonia class, atonement, fellowship, regeneration, bless,* and the list goes on.

We can easily forget that the local church is meant primarily to be a place where Christ followers come to encourage and equip one another, to go out and love as Christ loved. It's a greenhouse for growing saplings to be planted everywhere, to flourish and reproduce.

The local church is not the end, it's only the beginning.

Chapter 16

RECONNECTING WORSHIP WITH SOCIAL JUSTICE

When nine church members were gunned down in The Emanuel African Methodist Episcopal Church of Charleston, my heart hurt and my body burned with anger. The senseless, racist attack was humanity at its worst. I wondered how anything good could ever come out of this.

Then something beautiful happened. The Sunday after the mass killing, churches across Charleston canceled their services. Instead of meeting in their separate buildings that Sunday, pastors told their people they would worship as one with the members of Emanuel AME Church—sitting and praying with their brothers and sisters who are going through life's darkest night.

That Sunday so many people showed up at AME, there

wasn't enough room to fit in the building. Thousands of people—of every race—gathered in and around the church and worshipped as one.

Something like heaven on earth happened that Sunday—justice was connected with worship.

On a recent Sunday, my wife and I met our son Spencer in Southern California to worship at the church whose staff he had joined. When we arrived, we were told it was Service and Serve Sunday. The idea was that everyone would worship together, then serve.

The pastors provided eighteen different opportunities to serve that Sunday, all focused on others in need in their local community or places far away. Bulging boxes of fresh produce were packed for the immigrants and the homeless nearby. Some filled shoe boxes with Christmas gifts for kids in Africa. Teenage girls packed hygiene kits for teenage girls in Haiti. Veronica, Spencer, and I helped bag forty thousand food packs for orphans in Ecuador.

Do you see what was happening that Sunday? Worship was connected with justice. It was good and biblical, like Jesus' description of the kingdom of God in Matthew 25.

Most Christians have never given much thought to the connection between worship and justice. Our worship is simply not structured that way in most churches. We are good at celebration and joy in worship, or at the cerebral in our teaching, but rarely do we make issues of justice a part of our worship.

True worship, however, points God's people toward justice. This pattern is clear from the beginning of Scripture to the end. Let me share a few examples.

The Patriarchs Connect Worship with Justice

Moses worshipped barefoot.

It was a scorching-hot Sinai day when Moses saw the bush burning. Realizing God was present, he dropped face-down in worship.

Then God spoke from the bush: *"Take off your shoes, Moses. Walk with my barefoot slaves. Take off your shoes, because you are no longer son of Pharaoh; you are my son, one with the poor."*

God's invitation extends to you: take off *your* shoes and walk the holy ground of a broken world.

Next God said to Moses, "Go to Pharaoh and say to him, 'This is what the Lord says: Let my people go, so that they may worship me.'"

Justice for the barefoot slaves freed them to worship!

This same theology of liberation leads God's people to free the poor from poverty, the sick from disease, the immigrant from racism. Sometimes we make biblical liberation only about freedom from sin, but that is an incomplete theology. A right understanding of worshipping God also connects worship with practical issues of social justice.

The Ancient Prophets Connect Worship with Justice

When God spoke through the prophet Micah, He clearly explained what kind of worship pleases Him—not offerings, not performance, but these three things: doing justice, loving compassion, and living humbly.[1]

We love to quote these words about worship, but will we live them?

In the middle of Israel's darkest nights, God spoke again, this time through the ancient prophet Isaiah, about right worship, saying, "I don't want your fake worship acts."[2]

God is saying, you sing and pray and preach sermons about these things, but are you actually doing them?

Jesus Connects Worship with Justice

From an early age we are taught in church about Jesus' moment walking on water, His moment with a short tax man, or His moment feeding five thousand. But the moment we talk little about is when He walked into a worship house, dramatically unrolled Isaiah's scroll, and read of His calling to care for the poor and the powerless. Jesus—from the very beginning of His ministry—sought to connect worshippers with justice.

This is Jesus' most neglected moment.

Then, in His final moments of ministry, Jesus reminded us that connecting worship with justice is not just a nice idea, it is vital to salvation itself. With His words, Jesus paints a picture of how heaven views the right kind of worship: "he will sit upon his glorious throne. All the nations will be gathered in his presence . . . I tell you the truth, when you refused to help the least of these my brothers and sisters, you were refusing to help me. And they will go away into eternal punishment."[3]

His point is troubling: if our worship before the throne of heaven fails to produce justice and compassion, the consequences are eternal.

Jesus' most pointed statement on this issue comes when He describes the most God-pleasing worship. He cites the Hebrew prayer the Shema (love God with all your mind, soul, heart, and strength), and then he alters—enhances—it by going further and connecting worshipping God with caring for your neighbor! "Love your neighbor as yourself."[4]

If in our worship we forget about our neighbor, then our worship is hollow and incomplete. Biblical worship points us toward our neighbor.

Now We Must Connect Worship with Justice

In worship, we must find solidarity with the poor.

A robust theology of worship connects worship with justice.

This section of the book has been a study of the relationship between spirituality and justice—and in the church of today, this is unfortunately a strained relationship.

When I was young and new to the pastorate, I knew little of what spirituality really meant. I was taught that it was primarily about singing songs and praying nice prayers and confessing moral shortcomings in small groups. It was a theology of personal morality.

It always felt a bit lacking, even disingenuous.

For the most part, we live with an out-of-balance spirituality—heavy on the side of personal morality, feather light on the side of justice. .

Not that personal purity is not important. But if all we do in our small groups is talk about our personal shortcomings and personal aspirations, then our spirituality turns rather self-absorbed.

What is needed is a spirituality heavy on justice. Everybody thrives on challenge. We want a mountain to climb.

What if instead of being so self-focused we challenged each other to find innovative ways to promote the disadvantaged and end discrimination in our workplaces? Or change the unjust structures in our community? What if we held each other accountable to spending more time with the immigrant neighbor next door?

That's the kind of justice hill every person of God needs to climb.

My point is, justice and mercy are not nice things to do in addition to worship; they are fundamental to worship.

Every week when we worship, through the spirit of God, we are connected to fellow worshippers around the globe. Our voices and lives become one with those of the poor and the oppressed everywhere who are also lifting prayers to God.

What most of us don't think about each Sunday is that our worship makes us one, for example, with the barefoot poor of Liberia.

Each Sunday, people of the Mano tribe in Liberia gather in my good friend Eleazar Gbangan's church to worship. Eleazar wrote me recently, pleading, "Please bring more shoes to Liberia. The women and children in my church are going to the village outhouse barefoot . . . and contracting Ebola. They are stepping in the dysentery, urine, or vomit of people sick with Ebola. Two women in my church have already died from contracting Ebola in the outhouse. Please bring shoes quickly."

So when you worship this Sunday, remember you are

worshipping with the Mano tribe of Liberia, who walk precariously barefoot to the village outhouse.

And if your worship is biblical, then you will be drawn to responding to your fellow worshippers in their desperation.

That is why the Sunday after receiving Eleazar's letter, I asked the people of our church for their shoes, on a day we called Barefoot Sunday. I told them I needed their shoes for the Mano people in Eleazar's church. People took off their shoes, worshipped barefoot, and left eight thousand pairs of shoes on our stage for their fellow worshippers in Liberia.

Now do you see how worship is inseparably connected to justice?

For God So Loved the World . . .

The large churches in our country give much attention to worship programs and presentations. They hold rehearsals and have production managers. They purchase million-dollar sound systems and pump in fog. They satellite and video-venue and image-magnify . . . but practically none are known for being bastions of social justice.

It's practically the opposite. The past-generation Christian avoided the term; many actually despise the words *social justice*. As a result, our words of worship are silent on the subject, and we promote a brand of spirituality that will always be deficient, incomplete. And then we wonder why people remain spiritually hollow and shallow. We wonder why the next generation is abandoning the church.

Maybe our vision has been too small-minded. We take Jesus' grand words "For God so loved the world" and never for a moment believe that God actually loves the world! But when Jesus spoke those iconic words, He meant it.

He loves the ten-year-old sweatshop worker in Bangladesh. He loves the girls of Thailand sold for sex. He loves Lincoln from Trinidad, who kept being stopped by the police. He loves the immigrants, all of them. He loves the Liberian three-year-old who sat alone and cried herself to sleep for a week after her parents died from Ebola. God loves the world He made. He has not abandoned it. And He put you here to keep it, restore it to its original pristine condition, and heal the land and His precious people.

Isaiah opens our eyes to God's plan for our world and makes the critical connection between authentic worship and social justice:

> Tell my people what's wrong with their lives.
>   They're busy, busy, busy at worship, and love
>   studying all about me.
> Do you think this is the kind of fast day I'm after: a
>   day to show off humility? [. . .]
> This is the kind of fast I'm after: to break the chains
>   of injustice, get rid of exploitation in the work-
>   place, free the oppressed.

What I'm interested in seeing you do is: sharing
your food with the hungry, inviting the homeless
poor into your homes, putting clothes on the
shivering ill-clad.[5]

God says, "I want you to care about more than just your
own private spirituality." According to Isaiah, true religion
involves the pursuit of justice and the practice of mercy toward others.

When Isaiah writes about right worship, he points toward justice.

When Micah explains the life best lived for God, he
says to act justly.

When Amos drafts poetic prose about worship, he says
to let justice flood our lives and this world.

The trouble is, worship in the Bible is never solely a ver-
tical act; it requires a horizontal love to all around.

The brilliant St. Patrick used to pray a prayer that reminds all of us that every breathing soul is a precious child
of God, and God is present in their lives. My friend Leeland
has put his prayer to music:

Above and below me,
Before and behind me,
In every eye that sees me,
Christ be all around me.

May Christ be all around you.

May you see Him in the eyes of the immigrant who stands in front of a hardware store, hoping for work.

See Him in the life of the single mother holding her child close.

See Him in the faces of the young biracial couple who comes to worship filled with timidity, unsure they will be wanted and welcomed.

See Him in the man who sits alone because his wife has walked out on him and their children.

See Him in the teenage girl with the many scars on her arm.

See Him always.

May Christ be all around you.

Chapter 17

JUSTICE STARTS NOW

On some days the trouble in this world seems overwhelming, too much for one person to do anything about. But I write to remind you that God wants to use your one and very important life to change all of this. You—yes you—can turn the tide. Start with the place and the issue of injustice or oppression that God puts in front of you, the one that keeps you up at night, bothers you deep at the core.

God empowers you as His agent of change. Not just the paid professional. Not just the nonprofit humanitarian. He uses ordinary, real people like you to make this world right.

Because only one force on earth can change the trajectory of an individual, family, neighborhood, city, or society—a person sent by God to turn it all around.

That's you.

A person like you, sent by God, is the only force that can change the downward spiral of a bitter person to a loving person, a broken family to a reconciling family, a racially divided community to neighbors who live as one.

You are the hope of the world.

And yes, of course, we know theologically Jesus Christ is the hope of the of the world, but without people like you doing the kingdom work of God, then all the good He has for earth stays in heaven. However, when your life touches the life of a person or community that is hopelessly spiraling, God uses you to be the hope of the world.

The preeminent social justice theologian Walter Brueggemann turns to the Moses story to make this point, that God needs a body: "divine resolve turns abruptly to *human agency* . . . 'come, I will send you to Pharaoh to bring my people, the Israelites, out of Egypt.' The outcome is a human agent who can act and dream."[1]

God needs a person like Moses. Like you.

This is your calling. This is your destiny.

You are the hope of the world.

When you see a certain trouble in this world, God will stop you in your tracks, He will weigh the need heavy on your soul. The calling and compulsion will be so strong you will want to quit your job or spend every last dollar to make it stop.

That's how you know you are living *collective faith*, when you are selflessly sacrificing, willing to risk your reputation, risk criticism, risk everything, in the pursuit of the common good and justice for all.

It might be ending the sex trade of girls, or becoming a voice for the racially marginalized, or using your medical background to help stop the spread of pandemics. You will know.

The problem is, sometimes we see the need, we hear the voice of God, . . . then we think, "I don't have the time, somebody else will intervene, I'm not an expert, I don't have enough money, what will my friends think of me."

And we end up doing nothing.

When the voice of God says, "This one is for you," do it.

And start in your own backyard.

Sometime we only hear about the trouble in faraway places like Calcutta and Cartagena and focus our attention there. And sometimes God will ask us to go far away. But God always wants you to start nearby. Begin seeing the inequity around you, and step in. Because the things we do globally to right the imbalances are only legitimate if we are first responding to the needs in our own community.

Change Makers Today

Today an army of change makers is rising up to turn the tide on oppression and injustice, on poverty and pandemics. Be inspired by their example. Join their causes. Or dig deeper and take up one of your own.

Giving Keys: www.TheGivingKeys.com

Caitlyn Crosby is inspiring a generation with discarded keys. It started when the Hollywood socialite tied her hotel room key on a string and hung it around her neck. Her moviemaking friends loved the raw jewelry.

A light switched on. She began collecting old keys. Next she hired the homeless on Hollywood Boulevard to stamp words on the keys like *Love*, *Hope*, *Courage*, *Believe*. And then she started selling them in places like Nordstrom.

Caitlyn has a message with her keys. "Only wear it until you meet someone who needs it more than you, then take off your key and hang it around their neck—to give them *courage*, to show them *love*, to help them *believe*."[2]

Something very biblical is happening through Caitlyn: she's repurposing, she's giving meaningful work and income to the homeless, and God's message of love and hope is spreading one key at a time.

I don't know how soon I will be able to give away the key around my neck. It says *Love*, and I need it every time I drive the freeway and someone starts tailgating me. I squeeze the key between my fingers and pray, "Love. Love them like Jesus, Palmer!" I even change lanes now and let them pass. I'd never done that before.

The Giving Key works.

Krochet Kids: www.KrochetKids.com

I love Krochet Kids' pithy motto, "Buy better and know who made it."

Kohl Crecelius learned to crochet in college, then convinced two friends they could make their own beanies for snowboarding in Big Bear and winter surf days in Huntington Beach.

On a trip to Africa they realized their one quirky skill—crocheting beanies—could be used for the good of an entire community. So they began teaching women in Africa and South America how to make the snug, warm beanies that surfers and snowboarders in So Cal love.

Their mission, Kohl says, is to flip the script on donor-based charity that only meets a short-term need, and re-imagine the way we help people rise out of poverty. Through things like apparel, we can empower local entrepreneurs in developing countries to create a new future for themselves, their families, and generations to come.

Kohl and his crochet-aficionado buddies were not wealthy or well connected. They simply turned a passion and a skill into a divine-purposed mission for good. So can you.

Live Love: www.WhatIsLiveLove.com

You don't have to be a young millennial or travel to faraway places to be a change maker; this kind of life starts in the neighborhood next door. Live Love is in my backyard in Chandler, Arizona. It's changing the way churches and Christians relate to the blighted neighborhoods in their own communities.

Live Love was founded by my colleague and friend Paul Gunther and his wife, Melinda, in Chandler, where it seems that most people—even Christians—resent immigrants. Rather than shunning new arrivals and urban poor, Live Love is going to them, sitting with them, hearing their stories, tutoring their children. They are making art and music together, teaching English, planting community gardens. Closing the distance.

Exodus Road: www.ExodusRoad.org

My friend Matt Parker founded Exodus Road after he traveled to Thailand when he was a high school pastor. Matt said he was floored by how young the girls for sale on the streets of Pattaya were.

Now in his mid-thirties, Matt quit his church to help

the girls sold for sex in Southeast Asia. He started Exodus Road to build a massive coalition of abolitionists to pull girls out of the brothels and karaoke bars and massage parlors.

I've been undercover with Matt in the seedy bars and the shady restaurants. He's making a difference. The mama-sans and pimps are being arrested. The girls are being rescued and set free. But Matt needs help. The fires are burning out of control and we need more brave people like Matt on the front lines.

African Bible Colleges: www.AfricanBibleColleges.net

My parents, Dr. J. W. and Nell Chinchen, have shown all of us it is never too late to follow God's dream for your life. At age fifty, they founded a Christian college in Liberia, because education is perhaps the most effective tool in empowering a people to thrive. At sixty, they founded a second college in Malawi. At seventy, they built a third college in Uganda. They are now in their nineties and recently boarded a plane for Liberia to reopen the college there after its closure during the Ebola outbreak.

Ideas for You

God works through individuals like you, not just large non-profits and global organizations. Here are a few places everyone can begin:

Start a Vlog (Video Blog)

The YouTube generation has taken over the media. They prefer to view the world and interact through one-minute videos. So pull out your iPhone and start talking; start recording and editing and posting about all the things we can change for good.

Volunteer with a Nonprofit

Start your own nonprofit: yes you can. This week I'm meeting with Greg, whom I've known for years. Greg's in real estate and he has an idea. He's starting a nonprofit he wants to call A House for a Home. He wants Relators to advertise that when they sell a home, 10 percent of their commission will be used to build a home for a single mother in Africa, and he wants to ask the buyer and seller to all participate as well! "When you buy a house or sell a house, we will build a home." How do you like that?

Get on a Plane

Leave home. Leave the comfort of your suburban neighbor-hood and church. God inspires as we go.

Plant a Garden

Make sustainability a habit. Promote fair trade. Become a social entrepreneur who profits for good and invests in communities that produce the good we consume.

And More . . .

Live simply so you can share more.

Collaborate over coffee. Pull colleagues and friends together to pool their best thinking and resources to make real change.

Slow down. Un-busy. Make time for the least and the left out.

AFTERWORD

Who will have your heart?

In the Liberian jungle, every kid knows the Heartman wants your heart. He comes in the darkness of night dressed in white. He's the grim reaper with a glow. He will haul you to the devil-bush in a burlap rice bag where the sacrifices are made by the grand devil and the witch doctor. So as I told you, at night kids run. You never walk in the dark jungle—you run.

The Heartman may be thousands of miles away in Africa, but he wants your heart, too. Never miss the fact that a battle wages for your heart. Your career wants your heart. Working out and eating out want your heart—your heart can obsess with a P90X routine as much as it can with sushi and steak. Your bank account wants your heart; so does your portfolio and real estate and 401(k). Your habits and addictions want your heart. Pleasure and leisure want your heart—manicures and pedicures and golf weekends and beach condos all want your heart. New cars and new outfits and new quads and new pumps want your heart.

And so does God in heaven.

This book has been a story about who will have your heart—your whole heart—not just half.

Giving God all your heart is not as easy as it sounds, because the world is filled with things and people and places that all want a piece of your heart.

But the God of heaven sent His son, Jesus, to capture your heart. He kept saying, "Love the Lord your God with all your heart." He knew well that there is a war for your heart. Yes, yours.

Maybe when Jesus grabs your heart He doesn't take it as much as He makes it better. He says it can be brand-new. He gives you a more tender heart, a heart that hurts when you see things around you that are not right. He fills you with compassion, like when you see a worried mother, a frightened teenage girl on the street, or a hungry Haitian father.

And the longer you walk with God the more your heart grows: stronger, better, more noble, more just. But you cannot grow this kind of heart on your own; it grows with every step you take with Him.

AFTERWORD

So He waits—He waits to walk the path of life with you. He waits for you to say two simple words, "Carry me." That's how the Liberians say it when they must go somewhere especially difficult, somewhere far. They leave off the *halfway* part and just say *carry me*. When a friend says that, you listen. You know they are in trouble, afraid, or feeling desperate and alone. *Carry me* implies *stay with me*. Don't leave me. I cannot do this alone.

A close friend will have only one answer: *I will carry you.* And so will your Father in heaven carry you.

ACKNOWLEDGMENTS

My deepest gratitude and love to all who had a part in this book:

Kathy Helmers, *literary agent*: for your relentless prodding to complete this book connecting spiritual formation and social justice.

Jonathan Merkh, *publisher*: for being a risk taker. You inspire me.

Becky Nesbit, *editor in chief*: for your extraordinary enthusiasm. It's contagious. And a million thanks for taking time to personally read and refine this manuscript. Your work is beautiful.

Jessica Wong, *editor*: for sharing your insane editing skills and brilliant insights.

Acknowledgments

Katie Sandell, *associate editor*: for your rigorous attention to detail and constant encouragement.

Jim Chaffee, *booking agent*: for being a great friend and Barefoot Tribe partner.

NOTES

Introduction: Love and Justice

1 Psalm 122:8.

2 Jeremiah 29:7.

3 Jeremiah 29:5–6.

4 Proverbs 31:9 TLB.

5 Isaiah 58:6–7.

6 Micah 6:8.

7 Amos 5:24.

8 Luke 4:18.

Chapter I: Why Social Justice Matters

1 Walter Brueggemann, *Journey to the Common Good* (Louisville, KY: Westminster John Knox Press, 2010).

2 James 2:18 NLT.

3 Mark 14:7, author paraphrase.

4 Vikas Bajaj. "Fatal Fire in Bangladesh Highlights the Dangers

Notes

Facing Garment Workers," *New York Times*, November 25, 2012.

5 Jeffrey Sachs, *The End of Poverty* (New York: Penguin Books, 2006).

Chapter 2: Carry Me Halfway

1 Mark 12:30-31.

2 1 Peter 2:2 MSG.

3 Timothy Keller, "What Is Biblical Justice?" *RELEVANT Magazine*, August 23, 2012. www.relevantmagazine.com/god /practical-faith/what-biblical-justice.

4 Richard Stearns, *The Hole in Our Gospel* (Nashville: Thomas Nelson, 2009), 17–18.

5 Henri Nouwen, *The Wounded Healer* (New York: Image/ Doubleday, 1990), 81.

6 Shane Claiborne, *The Irresistible Revolution* (Grand Rapids, MI: Zondervan, 2006), 127.

7 Isaiah 61:8.

8 Luke 1:47–55 The Message.

9 Luke 16:19–31.

10 The 6:8 Project blog. https://the68project.wordpress.com /2015 /04 /29/aspiring-difference-maker-my-haiti-story-part-iii.

PART I: PASSION STAGE: THE QUEST FOR PURPOSE

1 Matthew 25:35.

2 James W. Fowler, *Stages of Faith: The Psychology of Human Development and the Quest for Meaning* (New York: HarperOne, 1985), 62.

3 Sharon Daloz Parks, *The Critical Years: Young Adults and the Search for Meaning, Faith, and Commitment* (San Francisco: Harper & Row, 1986), 30.

NOTES

Chapter 3: Justice Calling
1 Isaiah 58, James 1:27.
2 Ecclesiastes 4:1.

Chapter 4: Dream Life
1 Erwin Raphael McManus, *Wide Awake: The Future Is Waiting Within You* (Nashville: Thomas Nelson, 2008).
2 Scot McKnight, *One.Life: Jesus Calls, We Follow* (Grand Rapids, MI: Zondervan, 2010).
3 Jeremiah 29:11 The Message.
4 Joel 2:28.
5 Luke 1:18–19.
6 Luke 1:29–34.
7 *Les Misérables*, screenplay by Alain Boublil and Claude-Michel Schönberg, directed by Tom Hooper, based on the novel by Victor Hugo. Universal Pictures, 2012.

Chapter 5: Write a Million Words
1 Malcolm Gladwell, "Complexity and the Ten-Thousand-Hour Rule," *The New Yorker*, August 21, 2013.
2 Malcolm Gladwell, *Outliers: The Story of Success* (New York: Little, Brown and Company, 2011).

Chapter 6: Make Waves
1 From Matthew 5:5–10.

Chapter 8: YOLO
1 Palmer Sunset Cliffs. Youtube: https://www.youtube.com/watch?v=eX2wAAYw2Uc.

PART 2: AUTHENTIC FAITH: THE LONGING FOR AUTHENTICITY
Chapter 9: Racism and the Real You

1 Austin Channing "Justice, Then Reconciliation" September 2014, http://austinchanning.com/blog///justice-then-reconciliation.
2 Galatians 3:28 NLT.
3 Isaiah 56:10, author paraphrase.
4 John Perkins, *Let Justice Roll Down* (Grand Rapids, MI: Baker Books, 2006), 66.
5 Matthew 5:44–46.

Chapter 10: Participation Promotes Authenticity

1 Romans 10:15.

Chapter 11: From Institutional to Authentic

1 Fast Facts about American Religion, Hartford Institute. http://hirr.hartsem.edu/researchfastfacts/fast facts.html.
2 Frank Viola and George Barna, *Pagan Christianity?: Exploring the Roots of Our Church Practices* (Carol Stream, IL: Tyndale Momentum, 2008), 216.
3 Mark 14:36 NLT.

Chapter 12: Out of Boxes of Shame

1 *New York Daily News*, "Pope Francis Washes Feet of Prisoners, Baby during Holy Week Ceremony." Associated Press. April 4, 2015.

PART 3: COLLECTIVE FAITH: THE PASSION FOR JUSTICE

1 Jeremy Rifkin, *The Empathic Civilization: The Race to Global Consciousness in a World in Crisis* (Los Angeles: Tarcher, 2009).
2 Luke 18:18–23 MSG.
3 Fowler, *Stages of Faith*, 200.
4 Ibid., 200.

5 James Fowler, *Faithful Change: The Personal and Public Challenges of Postmodern Life* (Nashville: Abingdon Press, 2000), 66.

6 Leonard Sweet. *Soulsalsa: 17 Surprising Steps for Godly Living in the 21st Century* (Grand Rapids, MI: Zondervan, 2000), 114.

7 Isaiah 59:7.

8 Amos 5:21–22.

Chapter 13: Jesus Justice

1 www.panapress.com/Mandela-arrives-in-Malawi-for-talks-with-Muluzi—12-459697-127-lang1-index.html.

2 From Matthew 25.

3 Dr. Martin Luther King, Jr., "Letter from a Birmingham Jail." April 16, 1963. African Studies Center—University of Pennsylvania. www.africa.upenn.edu/Articles Gen/Letter Birmingham .html.

4 Mona Eltahawy, *Headscarves and Hymens*, 81

Chapter 14: Justice Conversion

1 Alan Cowell, "After Years, Vatican Says Galileo Was Right: It Moves," *New York Times*, October 31, 1992, pp. 1, 4.

2 Brennan Manning, *The Ragamuffin Gospel* (Sisters, OR: Multnomah Publishers, 2005), 51.

3 Jessie Simpson, The Grove, Chandler, Arizona, October 2010.

Chapter 15: Outward-Focused Lives

1 Michael Frost, *The Road to Missional: Journey to the Center of the Church* (Grand Rapids, MI: Baker Books, 2011), 95.

2 Genesis 12:2.

Chapter 16: Reconnecting Worship with Social Justice

1 Micah 6:8.

2 Isaiah 58 The Message.

Notes

3 Matthew 25:31–32, 45–46 NLT.

4 Mark 12:30.

5 From Isaiah 58 The Message.

Chapter 17: Justice Starts Now

1 Brueggemann, *Journey to the Common Good*, 112.

2 Author conversation with Caitlyn Crosby, February 2015, Chandler, Arizona.

ABOUT THE AUTHOR

Palmer Chinchen, PhD, is lead pastor of The Grove in Chandler, Arizona, a young, innovative, and rapidly growing congregation. Before that he served as a college pastor at Wheaton Bible Church in Wheaton, Illinois, and to Biola University students in La Mirada, California.

Palmer was raised deep in the jungle of Liberia, where the only way in and out was by prop plane. He later returned to Africa with his wife, Veronica, and four sons, where he taught spiritual development and practical theology at African Bible College in Malawi and Liberia.

A rising voice in the missional movement, Palmer is passionate about creating a fresh desire among Christians to reach a hurting world. Drawing from his experiences growing up in Africa, Palmer writes and speaks with authority about the most desperate needs facing our world today. His memories of the ravages of war and disease, as well as the effects of extreme poverty, fuel his desire to see us change what is not right in our world.

A little more than ten years ago, Palmer moved with his family to the booming Phoenix East Valley city of Chandler to help plant a church. Over Palmer's time at The Grove, the church has experienced exponential growth, and a tribe of Christ followers has gathered who tirelessly work together to stop injustice, end extreme poverty, and share the love of Christ.

Palmer holds a PhD in educational studies from Trinity Evangelical Divinity School in Illinois and a BA and MA in intercultural studies from Biola University in California.

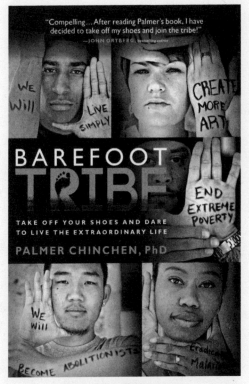